GOVERNMENT

AND POLITICS

IN AFRICA

SOUTH OF

THE SAHARA

STUDIES IN POLITICAL SCIENCE

RANDOM HOUSE   NEW YORK

Thomas R. Adam

New York University

Third Edition, Revised

GOVERNMENT

AND POLITICS

IN AFRICA

SOUTH OF

THE SAHARA

First Printing, 1959
Revised Edition, 1962
Third Edition, Revised, 1965
© *Copyright, 1959, 1962, 1965, by Random House, Inc.*
All rights reserved under International and Pan-American Copyright Conventions. Published in New York by Random House, Inc. and simultaneously in Toronto, Canada, by Random House of Canada Limited.
Library of Congress Catalog Card Number: 64-25045
Manufactured in the United States of America by The Colonial Press Inc., Clinton, Massachusetts

CONTENTS

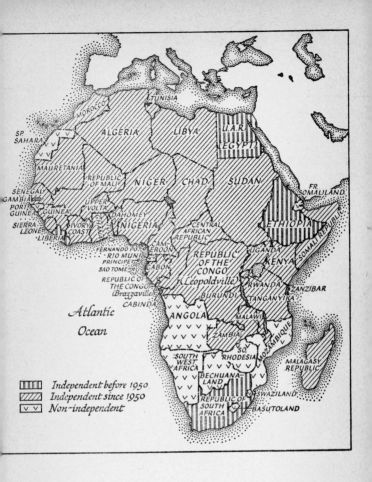

Independent before 1950
Independent since 1950
Non-independent

GOVERNMENT

AND POLITICS

IN AFRICA

SOUTH OF

THE SAHARA

ONE

++++++++++++++++++++++++++++

INTRODUCTION

Modern political institutions represent novel and perhaps alien creations to the bulk of the indigenous inhabitants of Africa south of the Sahara. Lack of continuity in African tradition may be attributed, in part, to European colonialism. At the time of the Western impact, African social organizations were already in a condition of dissolution. Nevertheless a breach was torn in African history by reason of the inability of the forceful intruder to understand the nature of the cultures brought under his dominance. Traditional boundaries were obliterated, language groups split between contending European masters, while the customary institutions of African society were denigrated by rulers who found them incomprehensible in terms of their own experience.

The African situation in the nineteenth and twentieth centuries may be described in terms of a clash of cultures. Political force was not dedicated to the maintenance and gradual development of social forms, as in Western lands, but rather to a reconstitution of basic human relationships. That this was largely unintentional on both sides hardly mitigated the severity of change. The British in Kenya, for example, undermined the cohesion of Kikuyu society by land transfers in fee simple, an application of their own history they were almost powerless to avoid. Western legal and political systems, essential to the social consciousness of the European, proved dangerous poisons to the African body politic.

What has had to be reconciled within a hundred-year period is the whole history of Western organization, political, economic, and ideological, and the total experience of the African peoples, divergent in isolation. This situation has had to be resolved not by compromise and equal exchange but through dominance, subordination, and finally rebellion. In order to comprehend the differences in historical experience that separate Europe from Africa, it is well to recall the evolution of Western government through armed lordships to the autocratic régimes of the national kings and thence to the oligarchies and administrative bureaucracies preceding and accompanying the rise of representative government. In contrast, ancient African government seldom based itself on the organization of physical force. An outstanding student of African affairs, Lord Hailey, points out:

It is rare to find in British colonial Africa any instance in which the indigenous form of rule previously in force could be described as autocratic, and there are not many cases in which it could be described in a strict sense as authoritarian. It was a prevailing characteristic of the indigenous system of rule that whether power was vested in the hands of individual chiefs or of a ruling class, these had (unlike the absolutist régimes of a certain stage in European history) no machinery by the use of which they could impose obedience to their orders. They may in many cases have been able to rely on the support of religious sanctions, but in the last resort the real sanction lay in their ability to secure the acquiescence of their traditional advisers and ultimately of the community itself.[1]

Systems of government in tropical Africa today are instruments of a projected future, with foundations resting neither on general consent nor the continuity of tradition. Accordingly, specific governmental systems may be described and classified in terms of the apparent purpose the political order was designed to forward. This purpose may not always be identical with avowed objectives. Official bodies sometimes choose to operate under the shadow of a myth, a private form of truth essential to the survival of some ruling group.

European Dominance. One primary classification of African governments is the political order constructed to ensure the dominance of Western standards, interests, and personnel. The Union of South Africa, under Afrikaner Nationalist control, constitutes the prime example. Public force of every kind is concentrated in the hands of a minority in defense of an ideology of which the minority, itself, is the sole interpreter. *Baaskap,* that is, white bossism, represents in its crudest manifestation the use of politics to perpetuate the clash of cultures. A higher mystique would elevate it to a mission of civilization in the hands of an elect. In any case it represents a political organization geared to rule through command, in place of the more general Western concept of government through direction and discussion.

Another form of this general classification is to be found in the Portuguese provinces of Angola and Mozambique. In this area government seeks to resolve the clash of cultures, at least in theory, by the total subordination of indigenous patterns to the European model. According to the Portuguese constitution "the overseas provinces are an integral part of the Portuguese state." [2] In consequence European standards and interests control the direction of social and economic development. Political government provides the authoritative force needed to transform African society to suit European patterns. To the credit of Portugal it may be said that race and color prejudices are combatted. While the African is not denied theoretical equality, he is free to seek advancement only in terms of a Western dictated culture. In the meantime political force imposes on the indigenous community the naked will of a European master.

Neither South Africa nor the Portuguese African provinces have their forms of government wholly conditioned by a purpose of white dominance. The rights of the European element of the population as against officialdom have to be taken into account. Two levels of political organization may be said to exist: one intra-European, with some aspects of freedom and representation derived from Western history; the other intercultural, based on rigid authoritarianism.

It is perhaps helpful to visualize these particular governmental structures as lying outside the main Western tradition. Despite preservation of Western forms, the political
order is that of a conquering minority bound together by
an overwhelming need to exploit and dominate indigenous
resources and peoples. They are probably unstable régimes
feebly rooted in past experience and subject to ever increasing pressures from the flood of history.

Reconciliation of Multiracial Societies. A second form of
governmental classification centers around the reconciliation of multiracial groupings. Settler colonies, where Europeans and Asians have taken root for several generations,
claim with some justification that African citizenship can
no longer be associated with a single race. If European
domination is considered inadmissible as a long-term basis
of rule, then equitable arrangements must be concluded to
guarantee each element of a plural culture the freedom
and means to fulfill its functions. Majority control is considered unsuitable for communities in which economic
advancement remains almost wholly dependent on the
activities of minority groups of European and Asian origin.

A political order designed to reconcile different racial
groups into a single community offers an apparent solution
to problems encountered in these settler colonies. A basic
requirement is that government should precede and in fact
create the political state, in the sense of a community of
interests. This involves government in a role independent
of majority will until the consummation of social unity. In
this respect European metropolitan governments have still
a part to play as arbiters of colonial societies. A new experiment intended to achieve multiracial harmony was
launched with the creation of the Federation of Rhodesia
and Nyasaland. The United Kingdom government renounced direct responsibility in favor of a local régime
drawn from the self-governing colony of Southern Rhodesia and the Colonial Office territories of Northern Rhodesia and Nyasaland. While delegating responsibility and

accepting a watching brief over the progress of social union, the British parliament and people retained the power to foreclose the experiment by breaking up the Federation or arresting its progress toward Dominion status.

The Federation declared its purpose in the preamble to its constitution:

And whereas the association of the Colony and territories aforesaid in a Federation under Her Majesty's sovereignty, enjoying responsible government in accordance with this Constitution, would conduce to the security, advancement and welfare of all their inhabitants, and in particular would foster partnership and co-operation between their inhabitants and enable the Federation, when those inhabitants so desire, to go forward with confidence toward the attainment of full membership of the Commonwealth.

Partnership, unfortunately, remains a vague concept lacking any agreed definition of the roles of the European, Asian, and indigenous elements of the population. It has been cynically described as the relation between a horse and its rider with the African as mount and the European in the saddle. Nevertheless the forms of political organization within the Federation were to some extent determined by an obligation to achieve racial harmony in a recognized pluralistic society. The sanction of sovereign power in the hands of the United Kingdom parliament guaranteed the exercise of political authority in accordance with the constitution. Constituent elements, both European and African, composing the indigenous power structure, have had to plead their case before the British government acting in a more than theoretical capacity as constitutional sovereign. Dissolution of the Federation has proved the final judgment.

An older method of ordering justice in multiracial communities is based on direct colonial hegemony. Nowadays this might be described as a suzerainty of conscience on the part of the peoples of the old empires. Political authority prevails over economic influence or social control as the principal instrument for the resolution of a clash of cultures. For the time being such authority must be based outside the divided communities, standing relatively above the particular concerns of any one segment of the population. It should not be forgotten that throughout the greater part of tropical Africa multitribalism rather than multiracialism is responsible for the language and cultural barriers separating the population into suspicious and often hostile groupings.

The manner in which a European state accepts responsibility for multiracial and multitribal colonies reflects the governmental habits and social ideals prevailing at home. The British are great constitution builders, plying their craft in Kenya, Zanzibar, and elsewhere with considerable virtuosity. France deals in broad humanistic strokes, appealing to a cultural experience and interests shared in common to combat racialism and tribalism.

Transition from Colonial Rule. Another type of tutelage, that of preparation for independence, determines governmental developments in several African regions. Until quite recently eventual abdication has not been a generally accepted objective of colonial rule among European powers. Britain, however, has long pursued the aim of having her colonies drop as ripe fruit from the tree of political subordination to plant themselves in the shade of voluntary association. France's 1958 constitution established a "community of states" to administer themselves and manage their own affairs democratically and freely. Though all sub-Saharan African states controlled by France opted for independence under the provisions of the 1958 constitution, an initial decision to remain within the Community proved transitory. Economic ties and cultural sympathies have proved more realistic bonds than the mystique of an outmoded Community.

A clear statement of British colonial policy is to be found in the Colonial Office Report of 1947-48: "The central purpose of British colonial policy is simple. It is to guide the colonial territories to responsible self-government within the Commonwealth in conditions that ensure to the people both a fair standard of living and freedom from aggression from any quarter." [3] Political structures intended to foster such conditions must be designed along opportunistic lines in each separate area. From the rag bag of British constitutional history, where no political device is ever wholly discarded, the most ingenious governmental costumes have been tailored to fit the personalities of the emergent states.

To British eyes, a major obstacle in the path to self-government is an already established monopoly of power in the hands of some minority group. In the words of former Prime Minister Eden, "self-government is dependent on the transfer of power to the people and not only to a minority of the people concerned." [4] The self-governing colony of Southern Rhodesia, where a settler minority imposes its own political terms in absence of true representation of the indigenous majority, constitutes an outstanding example of this problem.

Independent African States. Before 1960 few African peoples located south of the Sahara had won recognition as independent nation-states. If Ethiopia and the Sudan are excluded as border states, Liberia, Ghana, and Guinea, with a total population of less than 10,000,000 represented independent Black Africa until the fateful year of 1960. Then the floodgates of freedom opened, permitting 24 sub-Saharan peoples to win recognition as independent nation-states. By 1964 the roster of free peoples included Ghana, Cameroon, Togo, Malagasy, Congo (Leopoldville), Dahomey, Niger, Upper Volta, Ivory Coast, Chad, Congo (Brazzaville), Gabon, Central African Republic, Senegal, Mali, Guinea, Nigeria, Sierra Leone, Tanganyika, Uganda, Malawi, Mauretania, Somalia, Rwanda, Burundi, Kenya, and Zanzibar in addition to the two African states, Liberia and Ethiopia, whose independence pre-dated the twentieth century. Northern Rhodesia will achieve full independence before 1965 under the name of Zambia.

To some extent the forms of government adopted have maintained the general pattern evolved under colonial domination. African communities have contented themselves in the initial stages of freedom with the operation of basically Western systems by and through African personnel. Consequently, patterns of governmental structure for an independent Black Africa may not yet be considered established. Multiracial communities have to reconcile the political authority of majorities with social situations resulting from deep ethnic cleavages before stable forms of independent governments are likely to be achieved. Broad lines of economic development and social control even within predominantly African communities must precede any final selection from among competing patterns of political organization: those oriented toward the West, Soviet-inspired variations, or new designs rooted in cultural traditions and habits peculiar to the African continent.

TWO

◆◆◆◆◆◆◆◆◆◆◆◆◆◆◆◆◆◆◆◆◆◆◆◆◆◆

EUROPEAN

DOMINANCE

Before a governmental system can be examined and fairly evaluated, it is necessary to know who are the subjects of political authority, and whether political authority has been imposed on them by conquest, internal terror, or through acts signifying initial choice and continuing consent. In normal Western areas the subjects of a political régime constitute the bulk of the population forming a settled community with social organization and tradition usually antedating current governmental forms. In Africa, however, this is not always the case. Sometimes European and Bantu have appeared almost simultaneously in areas where the true indigenous peoples, Bushmen, Hottentots, or Pygmies, lived scattered in rudimentary social groupings.

THE REPUBLIC OF SOUTH AFRICA

The Cape Colony, settled by the Dutch in the seventeenth century and later taken over by the British, constituted such an area. Hottentot society presented as trifling an obstacle to European settlement as did the aboriginal Bushmen in Australia. Accordingly the resulting society, in its political as well as its social and economic aspects, was practically wholly European. In fact it was not until the mid-nineteenth century that the Kaffir tribes ceased to be dealt with under treaties similar to the frontier arrangements made with American Indians by the United States government. The fact that it was originally designed for Europeans in undisputed control of territory they regarded as their own remains an important element in the structure of the South African state as it exists today. The subsequent "native" problem which has resulted in the European's living in his traditional home as an armed minority has been caused in part by restless expansion northward and eastward into areas already occupied by well-organized African societies. It has been greatly aggravated, however, by Bantu migrations southward, contesting the Europeans' claims to lands and domination. Whatever the final judgment of history may be as to who was there first with the best claims, Bantu or European, the psychological basis of the present Union of South Africa is the conception of the European as original and true owner of the land. In consequence the nine to ten million Bantu are regarded as invaders or, to reapply a Boer term, "outlanders" by the three million Europeans. Though it may seem illogical to observers from abroad, the Afrikaners as well as many of the English-speaking immigrants consider their condition one of perpetual siege from within. The political organs of government then are never conceived as a means of uniting a territorial population in common action. They are viewed rather as a means of defense for white, Christian civilization threatened in its own homeland by overwhelming numbers, stamped irreconcilable enemies by their very color.

The dual character of South African government—the organization of its "own" people in representative, free institutions while autocratic rule is maintained over two-thirds of the population lacking rights for ethnic reasons—strains the logic of political explanation, at least in Western, non-Communist terms. It is perhaps easier to accept it as an unfortunate accident of history.

Sovereign Independence of South Africa. In the past the total responsibility of the government of the Union of

South Africa for the conduct of the country's internal and external affairs has been clouded in the eyes of some outside observers by the British connection. A theoretical constitutional suzerainty claimed by the wearer of the British Crown as token of membership in the British Commonwealth has given an appearance of involvement by the United Kingdom government in South African affairs. This viewpoint, generally speaking a misconception, has been rendered wholly nugatory by repudiation of Queen Elizabeth II as sovereign of South Africa in consequence of the result of a referendum held in October 1960. The new Republic of the Union of South Africa will in future stand before the world shorn of formal political ties to the United Kingdom, and to the Commonwealth that denied it re-entry. Economic pressure, of course, remains an indirect means of oversight. Up to the present the South African economy has depended for its growth on a continuing stream of capital investment from outside sources, principally London and New York.

Constitution of the Union of South Africa. By the South African Act of 1909 the British parliament gave constitutional form to the present Union. The Statute of Westminster of 1931 added freedom from United Kingdom interference. The South African legislature, itself, asserted the independent status of the Union by re-enacting the British-sponsored constitution as a law of the Union under the title of the Status of the Union Act of 1934. Amendments to the constitution could be enacted as ordinary legislation with the exception of what became known as the "entrenched clause." This provision barred any subsequent law disenfranchizing the colored electorate of the Cape Province for racial reasons, unless the law was passed by a two-thirds majority of both houses sitting together. In 1956 the Nationalist administration overcame this obstacle by a constitutional amendment which altered the numbers and composition of the senate, thereby creating a two-thirds majority for their party in a joint session. It may now be claimed that the sovereignty of the legislature over the constitution is, at least, legally assured.

Nature of the Union. South Africa is not a federal state. The Cape of Good Hope, Natal, Transvaal, and the Orange Free State constitute four provinces bound together in a legislative union. Sovereignty, political as well as legal, resides in the government of South Africa.

The titular head of the Union, formerly a governor-general, chosen by the government of the day but commissioned by the British sovereign, is now a president selected by the current administration. The executive organ of government consists of a prime minister, appointed from the leadership of the majority party in the legislature by the president, and such ministers as are subsequently selected to hold cabinet rank.

The legislature is composed of a house of assembly of 160 members elected on a constituency basis and a senate, now numbering 89, of which 71 are elected by the provinces and 18 nominated by the executive. Few vestiges of non-European representation survive. The seven European spokesmen previously supposed to represent African interests and viewpoint in the Parliament of the Union have been declared unnecessary in view of the régime's policy for the establishment of separate Bantu states. Only the Colored population of the Cape, though struck off the general voters' roll in 1956, maintain precarious indirect representation pending clarification of the Nationalists' views as to their political future.

The appellate division of the supreme court may rule, and has ruled, laws of the Union as well as acts of the executive unconstitutional. Since the overcoming of the "entrenched clause," however, the Union parliament appears in a position to reverse any court ruling by ordinary legislative procedure.

Provincial Councils. In each of the provinces a single-house provincial council, elected on the same system as the central assembly, is constituted to legislate by "ordinances" on specified and delegated subjects. Education for European children, up to and including the secondary level, local public works, hospitals, and some forms of direct taxation are on the specified list. While the central government may and does delegate many responsibilities held to be of a local nature, no provincial ordinance may run contrary to a Union law. In addition, the central executive may veto any provincial ordinance. The practice of subsidies, particularly in the case of education and public works, ties provincial affairs securely to the policy decisions of the Union administration. Important social policies, especially those relating to native affairs, are entirely in the hands of the central government.

Perhaps the greatest distinction between a South African province and an American State lies in the fact that the chief executive officer of the province, the administrator, is appointed by the Union government. Executive power on matters within the scope of the provincial council is vested in an executive committee composed of the administrator and four members, elected for a term of years by the provincial council.

Political Issues on the European Level. Processes of democratic government—participation by the governed, decision-making subject to full and free discussion, and absence of arbitrary power—operate in South Africa only in terms of problems considered inter-European. Matters that concern the relationship of the races are handled on an altogether different level. However, a considerable part of the political controversy that has divided voting South Africans up to the present day has centered around European questions. Perhaps the oldest line of demarcation lies between the Afrikaans-speaking[1] and English-speaking inhabitants. Creation of the Union failed to obliterate the bitter memories of the Boer war and the Afrikaners turned to intensive political organization to assert their claims. Social and economic differences account in part for the split. Traditionally the Afrikaner is a farmer or, more accurately, owner of a plantation operated by Negro labor, while the English-speaking element congregates in the urban areas, monopolizing to some extent the processes of industry, mining, and trade. Within the last two decades, however, underemployment in the rural areas has brought many young Afrikaners to the cities where they have tended to fill the ranks of the police and administrative services or drift into semi-skilled clerical or technological employment. An Afrikaan middle class is now emerging but remains a long way behind its English rival in terms of financial power. The Afrikaner share of the national income has been estimated as one-quarter of the total, with farming still the main source of wealth.[2]

Lacking equality of economic power, Afrikaners have overcompensated in political terms. The Nationalist movement that has been used to rally a disciplined voting mass under an authoritarian party is a sorry thing in terms of twentieth-century cultural standards. It has been instrumental in reducing a branch of the Christian religion to an ethnic cult; in raising a derivative language as a barrier to the understanding of Western culture; in separating the Afrikaner folk from the mainstream of ethical and power relationships in the modern world. South Africa has neglected the need for social union, concentrating instead on the development of economic resources, particularly in the field of the extractive industries. With the tempting bait of profitable investment it may be possible to purchase a few more years tolerance from power blocs in the Western sphere sufficing to offset the resentment of the Asian-African peoples and the watching hostility of Soviet power. The English-speaking element of the population has not engaged itself in purposeful or coherent political organization; absorbed in moneymaking activities, it consistently neglected political developments until events took the power to intervene effectively out of its hands. Now a new generation of young Afrikaners has been isolated from everything but their own culture by politically oriented

educational systems manipulating the language barrier.
This leaves the non-Afrikaner stock a permanent cultural
minority subject to increasing discrimination as the tide
of Afrikaan nationalism rises. A decisive point in the
downgrading of the English-speaking segment was reached
by the South African Citizenship Act of 1949.[3] Up to that
time British subjects, at least of "white" origin, had entry
and residence privileges on the basis of a common nationality. The Act of 1949, however, set the same conditions
for entry and practically the same waiting period before
the grant of South African citizenship for immigrants from
Britain as from any other Western land. Perhaps more sig-
nificantly, the right of entry has been made a matter of
ministerial discretion, leaving the door open for Nationalist
administrations to bar whole categories of English-speaking immigrants for reasons of political, cultural, or religious prejudice. Further, the English-speaking citizen of
South Africa was given clearly to understand that the retention of a British as well as South African loyalty would
no longer be tolerated. It is difficult to estimate the lengths
to which the Nationalist movement may go in discriminat-
ing against an English minority. Economic envy as well
as fanatic nationalism may tempt demagogic politicians to
exploit a situation where all the political power lies on one
side and a great part of the wealth on the other.

An issue that still crosses lines between Afrikaners and
English is the degree of personal freedom for Europeans
that will be retained under Nationalist rule. It must be
said that the régime seeks to create an impression at home
and abroad that it is committed to the basic freedoms that
Englishmen associate with their unwritten constitution and
Americans with the Bill of Rights. Of course in South
Africa such freedoms only exist for Europeans and, in
the process of carrying out arbitrary rule over the natives,
government is apt to confuse its powers. The Suppression
of Communism Act of 1950, for example, can be considered primarily aimed at preventing organized political
resistance on the part of the Bantu. In application, how-

ever, concepts like "statutory communism," which includes
any behavior that can be interpreted as encouraging interracial controversy, strike hard at independent-minded
Europeans. A growing willingness on the part of the administration to interfere with the freedom of religious
worship augurs unhappily for the protection of the other
bastions of civil liberty—free speech, a free press, and
freedom from arbitrary arrest.

Political Parties and Movements. The Nationalist party
provides institutional form for the power ambitions of a
majority of the Afrikaans-speaking element. Viewed as a
political party it is ruthlessly organized, harshly disciplined
in its thinking, and dependent upon emotional loyalties
and even threats of force for its internal cohesion—the
shadow of the secret society, the Broederbond, from which
many of its leaders are still recruited, remains omnipresent.
A stirring of dissent within Nationalist ranks occurred in
1960 with the formation of the National Union, headed
by ex-Chief Justice Fagan and a former Nationalist member from South-West Africa, Japie Basson. However, the
attempted assassination of Prime Minister Verwoerd discouraged internal self-examination within Nationalist ranks.
In the 1960 referendum establishing a republic, the Afrikaans-speaking parties received a clear majority of 52
percent of the voters, the first occasion on which they
had obtained a mandate without recourse to a gerryman-
dered minority vote.

A substantial portion of Afrikaans-speaking voters,
amounting perhaps to 15 percent, are linked with the
bulk of the English-speaking element in a major opposition grouping, the United party. In regard to the basic
question of the maintenance of European supremacy, the
United party disagree with the Nationalists primarily on
questions of methods rather than objectives. On the issue
of *volkseenheid* (exclusive unity of the Afrikaner people)
the United party claim the more sophisticated aim, advocated in the past by Generals Botha and Smuts, of a com-

mon identity for all inhabitants of European stock, English
and Afrikaan alike. In 1959, 12 members of Parliament
elected in 1958 under the banner of the United party
broke their party affiliation and formed the Progressive
party. Though stopping short of the advocacy of political,
economic, or social integration of ethnic groupings, the
Progressive platform stood for a bill of rights applicable
to all inhabitants, as well as the establishment of reasonable
contacts between the races. The mild liberalism of this
group failed in its first test at the polls with the consequent elimination of the party as a political entity.

An older and more daring opposition party was formed
in 1953 when the Liberal party split off from the United
party. The Liberals may be described as a "conscience"
group, failing consistently at the polls in both local and
national elections, yet serving as witnesses to the outside
world that the European society of South Africa is not a
monolithic bloc frozen in a stasis of fear and prejudice.
Alan Paton, the Liberals' most prominent spokesman, ad-
vocates uncompromising opposition to Nationalist policies.
"My country and my people will never be free until the
Government is utterly destroyed." [4]

There are now no legal political organizations on a national level to express the views of the African majority.
After the Sharpeville shooting in March 1960, the African
National Congress was deprived of its tenuous rights to
legal recognition. With Chief Luthuli as president-general,
the National Congress had exercised dignity and restraint
in promoting the interests of its people in a spirit of Gan-
dhian nonviolence. A more radical organization, the Pan-
Africanist Congress under the leadership of Robert M.
Sobukwe, a university instructor, had commenced to at-
tract greater African support than the moderate National
Congress. Held responsible for the Sharpeville agitation,
Mr. Sobukwe was jailed and his organization outlawed.

Rule over Africans. As far as the Bantu is concerned and,
to a slightly lesser extent, the mulatto and the Asian, South

Africa is a police state where government means the arbitrary authority of officials. The twin pillars of subordination for the African are the native reserves (or Bantu areas, as they are now officially termed) and the Department of Native Affairs. By virtue of these two institutions more than two-thirds of the population are barred effectively from sharing in the economic, social, or legal rights of their European compatriots. The reserve system was started in early colonial times as a means of ensuring living space for tribal Africans threatened by destruction of their communal land-holding systems. Protective in its origins, it evolved into a means of attracting and containing reservoirs of native labor contiguous to European settlements. Varying policies were practiced by the English colonies and Boer states before the formation of the Union. An early opportunity to provide sufficient living space and enough development funds to permit true separation of the Bantu and European communities was missed, if it was ever feasible at all, in a plantation and industrial economy dependent on a plentiful supply of native labor. After formation of the Union, efforts to regularize the system on a wide enough basis to meet minimum needs of a growing Bantu population met with opposition from the provinces. The definitive Native Land and Trust Act of 1936 giving the Union government power to purchase additional land for Bantu use proved an inadequate compromise. By 1951 the reserves constituted around 13 percent of the nation's area. The census of 1951 reported approximately 3.6 million Bantu on the reserves and 4.9 million outside on European farms or industrial areas.

The governmental as distinct from the economic principle involved in the system is that the Bantu "belongs" in his designated areas. His existence elsewhere, either in terms of livelihood or basic personal rights, is by grace of the European authorities. This convenient fiction that the Bantu can choose to return to customary, relatively autonomous tribal life if dissatisfied with his place in European society serves as a legal and even ethical foundation for administrative tyranny. The physical impossibility of survival for even half the native population on their deteriorated farms is dismissed as due to inherent character faults resulting in bad farming practice. To an American observer, sensitive to past practices concerning Indian reservations, the fiction is brutally familiar though on a terrifying scale. However, the administration of Dr. Verwoerd has committed itself to a grandiose policy of creating "Bantustans"—Bantu states—which at some remote future date may become autonomous or even sovereign nations. Since the period of police rule under the state of emergency that followed the Sharpeville shootings, the Nationalist régime has pressed forward with the Bantustan concept for obvious political reasons. Through the appointment of locality chiefs invested legally with outrageous authority over the lives of the resident community, the administration is in a position to govern Africans indirectly with tribal brutality. Even the African who has remained within the reserve areas appears unwilling to submit docilely to this form of anachronistic savagery. In December 1960, the government closed off the Pondoland area in northeastern Cape province to all outside observers. Africans had risen against the government-appointed chiefs and engaged in guerrilla warfare with the armored cars and aircraft of the European police. From the economic point of view the Bantustan concept appears impossible. It envisages the confinement of nearly 10,000,000 Africans to 13 percent of the less desirable land in order that 3,000,000 Europeans may enjoy the remaining 87 percent, comprising industrial, mining, and the better farming areas with of course the transportation network. The Europeans would not only be undisputed masters of the physical resources but also of an African labor force superior in numbers but subordinate in every other particular.

Department of Native Affairs. Analysis of the administrative structure of government in the Union tends to the conclusion that the affairs of the Bantu population are adminstered by a government within a government. While Europeans enjoy access to at least ten departments of ministerial rank for their contacts with government, the Department of Native Affairs monopolizes control, with the exception of police and courts, over every aspect of native African life from labor conditions, through education, to tribal organization. Politically speaking, this has the merit of concentrating the area of arbitrary power mainly in the hands of one department and its minister. The European state escapes some of the overflow of autocratic power that might result from having its affairs administratively entangled with those of the Bantu. On the other hand the African majority finds every detail of personal and economic freedom at the mercy of a single authority. Only the courts, and to a lesser degree police administrators, can give any relief from the dictates of the Department of Native Affairs.

The Policy of Apartheid. Despite all that has been written and said of the policy of *apartheid* "separateness" in South Africa, it is difficult to translate this policy into the practices of the existing governmental system. As a declaration of intention the policy is clear enough, allowing rational argument on both sides in cultural, ethical, and scientific terms. Any attempt, however, to describe the present rule of the Bantu people as a logical application of an *apartheid* policy is bound to prove unsatisfactory. Value judgments on the theory of *apartheid,* though tempting to undertake, must accordingly be treated as outside the scope of a brief description of a working political system. A student of politics is entitled to accept the existence of a mystique held by a power group as an operative fact even though it fails to achieve logical correspondence with actual policies. Sometime in the future, evidence may appear that Nationalist administrations in the Union are making serious efforts to provide separate existence for the races, economically and culturally, but until such time arrives it is misleading to force the specific acts of native policy into an impossible pattern for the development of separate societies.

Framework of Native Laws. Deprived of anything but token participation in the legislative process and powerless to control administrative action, the Bantu population can be regarded in political terms as a subject people. The legislative structure devised to ensure their subjection is thorough and highly efficient. For purposes of analysis it may be divided into six groupings: labor laws, settlement laws, education acts, police and moral regulations, tribal organizations, and land laws.

The Industrial Conciliation Acts of 1954 and 1956 create separate codes for governing the organization of white and African labor. Mixed trade unions were uncommon before the Nationalist régime, but since 1956 they have become unlawful. To speak of an African trade union is perhaps to use a euphemism, as such bodies cannot obtain legal status. In fact it is unlawful for African workers to bargain with their employers except through the medium of a government official, while it is a criminal offense to organize or participate in a strike. A network of laws specifically applied to African labor prevents the African worker's leaving one employer to better himself without the permission of a labor bureau, or to leave one area for another without special permission. For an African to break a contract of employment is a crime, not a matter of civil action between himself and his employer. A further step is the progressive enforcement of a color bar decreed by government for various categories of employment.[5] Discrimination to this extent might appear excessive to American eyes even if applied to a minority group. In light of the fact that Africans constitute 53 percent of the workers in private industry it must be regarded as a major factor in the shaping of the economic and social life of the state. Arbitrary control by government of over half of the nation's industrial labor force makes the existence of a free enterprise society a questionable matter.

The tested police maxim, "keep them on the move," has been erected into a cardinal principle of control in dealing with the African masses. As almost two-thirds of the Bantu live outside their reservations, in addition to the considerable Colored and Asian groupings to be taken into account, the danger of settlement of specific areas by non-Europeans has greatly exercised Nationalist régimes. The Group Areas Act of 1950 and subsequent Native's Resettlement Act of 1954 legitimize the uprooting of non-European populations in order that they may be moved around at the will of the central government. A simple designation that a place is a "white area" suffices to destroy long-established African suburbs. Under these acts 50,000 persons lost title to homes and lands in the Johannesburg suburb of Sophiatown in favor of being transferred to a government settlement where they live as tenants at will. Another Johannesburg suburb, Pageview, settled by non-Europeans for fifty years with freehold permitted since 1937, was declared a group area for white occupation. This time Indians with commercial investments of several million dollars were the principal victims. As a foretaste of how political power can be employed to control the livelihood of an Indian merchant class, this legislation may prove particularly effective in discouraging educated Indians from associating themselves with the cause of their Bantu compatriots.

In the eyes of the European community, while an African majority may be held inconvenient it will always be manageable until it discovers some method of internal organization and cohesion. The greatest threat to white dominance up to now has been the growing numbers and ability of an African middle class. Even though denied access to economic power, might not this group steal a page from the Nationalist's own book, challenging European social and economic control by political action? This is the essence of the "black nationalism" used as a bugbear by Afrikaner nationalists to frighten the European population into solidarity. The root of the danger to white supremacy then lies in Bantu education. Up to 1953 native

education had been a provincial matter, with the central
government providing financial assistance from general
revenue. A start had been made toward furnishing facilities for Bantu elementary education although the main
burden was still carried by church and missionary schools
—4,827 of them to the government's 992.[6] By the Bantu
Education Act of 1953 the Nationalist government transferred control of the subject from the provinces to the
central administration. The Department of Native Affairs
assumed total control, separating the Union Department
of Education entirely from Bantu schooling. A complicated
system of school classifications forced church schools,
which aimed at being more than parochial training institutions, to surrender their properties to local communities.
With the Minister of Native Affairs now in control of the
bulk of physical facilities, financial support, teacher training and selection, curriculum, and registration of new
schools, Bantu education may be viewed as safely subordinated. To tidy up the situation the universities were
brought to heel, perhaps unfortunately at the cost of their
membership in the ranks of free scholarship. Mixed universities were forbidden and the type of higher education
to be granted to Bantus placed under ministerial control
by the Separate University Education Act of 1957. All that
is needed now to safeguard the situation, from the Nationalist point of view, is competent bureaucratic operation of the system to produce a sufficient supply of labor
suitable to an industrial culture without producing intel-
lectual heresies concerning equality, freedom, or justice.

One of the unavoidable drawbacks to a dual system of
government such as that of South Africa is that autocratic
power and representative government share the same enforcement agencies. The South African Police Force is a
body requiring explanation to American or western European readers. It is not controlled by local communities for
the purpose of sustaining local concepts of orderly social
life. Instead it is a paramilitary instrument of the central
government with a powerful intelligence arm, the Security

Police. A busy and efficient organization of a strength around 11,000, it has the onerous task of seeing that at least one-tenth of the total population, not excluding women and children, are convicted of crime every year.[7] It is obvious that to reach such an impressive total there must be a large number of laws available to break. The Urban Areas Act of 1945 gives the police blanket permission to arrest any native within an urban area should he fail to fall within one of four categories or be considered idle or undesirable. The former Pass System, now consolidated into Reference books, still provides unfailing opportunity for arrest should a Bantu venture into the streets without the necessary documents. Liquor laws, forbidding possession or consumption of hard liquor by Africans, require spirited enforcement. Morality statutes, forbidding mixed marriages or interracial sexual intercourse on any terms, involve considerable supervision of the private goings and comings of individuals of all racial groups. On a higher level, the Suppression of Communism Act makes the police attend practically every form of public meeting where non-Europeans might be present. In effect, the personal security of every African rests on the will of a police officer who can always find legal justification for arrest. As police policy is controlled by a single minister, incipient social discontent can be met by arresting key figures on routine charges.

Perhaps the most questionable assumption of power by the European state, at least in terms of its own values, is the arbitrary authority asserted by the Department of Native Affairs over tribal organization and social development within the Bantu areas. During the last few years the Nationalist régime has sought to restore the tribal chief to a position of real power over his fellow Africans. The Bantu Authorities Act of 1951 is the precursor of this policy, which is based on the claim that the European is a better judge of the future of the tribal society than the Bantu people themselves. As the chiefs are, of course, subject to the arbitrary control of the European bureaucrat, the ideal

African society is designed according to a strict Nationalist pattern. In the meantime the preservation of tribalism
conveniently removes the population of the Bantu areas
from participating in the expensive social welfare required
by more individualistic Europeans. It can also be used to
assist the police in their tireless efforts to save the Bantu
peoples from falling under the "wrong" type of leadership
proffered by educated Africans with unsuitable ideas.
Granted that the policy has much to commend it in terms
of economy and convenience, it does seem to create an unfortunate paradox in turning the Minister for Native Affairs, a pillar of European, Christian civilization, into the
most powerful advocate of tribal reaction in the length and
breadth of the continent.

In Africa men still live by the land, which provides a
surer form of security, more solid ties to family and kin,
than all the conflicting laws, policies, ideals, and even
technology of the European intruder. The true measure
of the European state's claim to be a just government,
even though not based on consent of the governed, must
be found in its relation to the Bantu people's use of land.
If it has helped the indigenous African to develop agriculture through the dissemination of educational and technological aids, if it has supplied essential public works and
capital development, then credit must be given for furnishing the tools that should permit the African to build his
own modern social structure. The degree to which the
European state has accepted responsibility for African economic and social progress is spelled out in the Report of
the Commission for the Socio-Economic Development of
the Bantu Areas (the Tomlinson Report of 1955). This
thorough investigation was carried out by men committed
to the *apartheid* mystique of the Nationalists; the latter,
as could be expected accepted the findings of the report
in principle. The Tomlinson Commission found catastrophic destruction of soil fertility continuing in the Bantu
areas. It put forward an interlocking plan of development
similar in scale to that of the Tennessee Valley Authority,

embodying bold schemes for mass education, new crops, afforestation projects, and a radical reform of land tenure to permit private rather than communal ownership. The minimum expenditures needed in the next ten years to avert disaster were estimated at about $300,000,000. Even if its recommendations were adopted in full, the Tomlinson Commission did not pretend that the Bantu areas could contain the natural increase of the Bantu people. Statistical projections for the year 2000 worked out in the report showed the Bantu still outnumbering the European in the so-called European areas.

The Nationalist administration, while praising the theoretical assumption of the report, rejected the major reforms recommended, particularly in respect to replacement of tribal land tenure by forms of individual ownership. The sum of approximately $9,000,000 designated by the government for essential developments in Bantu areas for the year 1956-57 failed to meet the minimum required to halt further deterioration, much less launch any climb toward improvement. When practical action necessitates the spending of tax money collected from European sources, the Nationalist government appears more skeptical of the realities of separate existence for the races than do many liberal idealists. The system operated by the European state is one of subjugation of the non-European peoples. While the mystique of *apartheid* is perhaps necessary to provide an ethical basis for European solidarity, it has up to now been largely disregarded in the framing of operative policies. Subjugation is simpler and less expensive.

South-West Africa. To some extent the Union government of South Africa has laid the whole range of its policies as ruler of African peoples open to world criticism through its retention of a mandate over South-West Africa. Proceedings in the United Nations, backed by decisions of the World Court, aimed at forcing South Africa to give account of her conduct in this area have been long drawn out and acrimonious. Both in terms of international law

and politics, however, it is becoming increasingly difficult
for the Union government to resist United Nations pressure. Turning a floodlight on South African practices
through United Nations investigations might prove disastrous to the finely balanced power of the European government throughout the whole Union. While inhabitants
of South-West Africa have probably benefited from connection with South Africa, at least in comparison with
their sufferings under former German régimes, a United
Nations Visiting Mission, using standards similar to those
employed in Tanganyika or Ruanda Urundi, would create
an international sensation. In the present condition of the
modern world, minority government such as practiced in
the Union of South Africa depends on the avoidance of
intervention in any form on the part of the more powerful
states.

Future of the Political System of the Union. The present
Nationalist administration may not be described as a mere
Party government willing to step down in the normal
course of political change. It has committed itself and
seeks to commit the whole European community to a program of racial domination from which there will be no retreat. In American terms it is turning political attitudes and
policies into "a way of life." The outside observer then is
obliged to estimate the viability of a whole constitutional
system rather than the duration of temporary policies.

Apart from unpredictable international developments,
there does not appear any obvious internal threat to the
immediate security of the present structure. However, in
the modern world economic considerations frequently
overturn political planning. Nationalist fervor cannot sub-
stitute for economic stability and growth in a community
that draws its livelihood from interconnection with and
dependence on the industrial economy of the West. The
Union of South Africa needs the confidence of investment
capital outside its borders to retain its present system, political as well as economic. Grounds for such confidence

differ somewhat from judgments that might be passed on
a government of racial dominance from ethical or historical points of view. Nevertheless they are based on esti-
mates of the likelihood of social stability being maintained
under the existing system for periods up to twenty-five
years. The quality of thinking shown by the Nationalist
party, with their fanatic devotion to racial symbols and
corresponding irresponsibility toward the economic structure of a modern industrial society, makes it questionable
whether they can long retain the support of Western export capital, either public or private. A crisis of confidence,
when it arrives, will entail revolutionary and unforeseeable
changes in the social structure. Outside investment in
South African industrial development is becoming increasingly a matter of political speculation.

Developments in 1960 seriously weakened public confidence in South African stability in responsible circles in
Britain and the United States. When Prime Minister Macmillan addressed the Nationalist parliament at Capetown
in February 1960, he warned of "the wind of change"
blowing through Africa that, unless heeded by the Nationalists, might "make it impossible" for the United Kingdom
to continue support of the Union "without being false to
our own deep convictions about the political destinies of
free men." This unprecedented bluntness by the visiting
British statesman was later echoed in a report by South
Africa's leading industrialist, Mr. H. F. Oppenheimer, to
the stockholders of the great Anglo-American Corporation
of South Africa Ltd. "The achievements of the past 50
years are certainly notable, but in present circumstances
no thinking South African can look to the future without
misgiving, and the feeling is widespread that new policies
are urgently needed if we are to build a truly united South
Africa. This mood is by no means confined to the political
opposition." [8]

Police brutality at Sharpeville, involving the death of
72 Africans and the wounding of 186 others, evoked an
unusual direct condemnation from the official organ of the

United States government. Denunciation by the Security
Council of the United Nations, though fitting into a more
accustomed pattern, added to the feeling expressed by one
South African of occupying a permanent position as "skunk
of the world." Behind constant affirmations that Afrikaners
will not be swayed by world opinion, however adverse,
lurks the uncomfortable fact that South African economic
development is the creature of the confidence of the outside investor. Responsible financial, if not necessarily governmental, circles in Britain and the United States possess
the power through adoption of a negative attitude to arrest
industrial development and, perhaps, transform the power
structure of South African society.

PORTUGUESE AFRICA

In terms of political analysis the present theory of government in South Africa may be accounted a comparatively
novel and somewhat vulgar heresy in a neo-Hitlerian style
of race worship. A contrary view may be taken of the governmental structure of Portuguese Africa, though the end
results in terms of European dominance over Africans is
perhaps identical. Overseas Portugal maintains the continuity of a majestic inheritance handed down from the
great Lusitan empire of the fifteenth to seventeenth centuries. It is probable that this impressive tradition has become increasingly inapplicable to conditions in the modern
world. Yet the fervor and logic that are still brought to its
defense possess a quality to Western eyes that distin-
guishes Portuguese aims from the white tribalism of their
southern neighbors.

By an Act of 1951, later confirmed by the Organic Law
of the Overseas Territories of 1955 the former colonies of
a Portuguese empire were made provinces of the Portuguese nation. This did not entail revolutionary changes in
political or social outlook. The old Lusitan empire stood
for a people or culture in motion rather than regions held

in tribute to a metropolitan center. Brazil remains a lasting tribute to the intercultural force of Portuguese expansion. The root of Portuguese dominance, then, is not ethnic pride or unabashed mercantilism but faith in a total religious, social, and political culture that transcends territorial and racial boundaries. The instrument of this culture is the state, at present the authoritarian, corporative, Portuguese state, based not on the consent of its inhabitants at home or overseas but rather on its competence to guard and maintain a specific culture. As in the case of South Africa, the heavy weight of arbitrary power rests eventually on the emotional illogic of a mystique to be weighed in the pragmatic terms of whether it is capable of survival in the modern situation.

Four principles constitute objectives and provide a framework for Portuguese African administration.[9] The first is political unity in terms of one government, one people, one law. This is perhaps easier to approximate in the case of Portugal than it might be in states that accord more serious consideration to representative democracy. The singleness of government is assured by the great powers of the president under the constitution. Both on its own account and through the Minister for Overseas Portugal, the executive can legislate for overseas provinces as well as control administration through appointed governors and governor-generals. An inspectorate system outside the chain of command of the provincial governor-generals further centralizes administrative control in the metropolis. The national assembly and the corporative chamber have legislative and advisory powers over overseas provinces under the constitution. In the present one-party state of modern Portugal such powers are not likely to be used contrary to the policy of the executive. The same may be said of the advisory bodies that the Organic Law of the Overseas Territory requires the Minister for Overseas Portugal to consult before he decrees legislation and settles administrative policy. The Overseas Council is basically a body of government-nominated experts who serve as the highest administrative and judicial tribunal for overseas affairs in addition to advising the minister. The Conference of Overseas Governors is just what its name implies, a conference meeting at the convenience of the minister, who presides over its deliberations. There is nothing then in the constitutional or juridical picture to destroy the harmonious unity of a government operating throughout its African territories with the classic simplicity of a Roman imperator.

Possessed of powers rivaling those of an imperial procurator, the governor-generals of Angola and Mozambique administer their provinces, responsible only to the central government in Lisbon. As might be expected in the "New State" of President Salazar, the principal restrictions on the exercise of independent authority by a governor-general lie in the field of finance, particularly in respect to balanced provincial budgets and the granting of concessions for plantations, mines, or commercial monopolies. From the governor-general a chain of command runs through district governors, appointed directly by the Overseas Ministry, to administrators and chiefs of post.[10] An advisory body called the Government Council constituted of officials and two elected members of the Legislative Council, selected by the governor-general, now aids in the preparation of the budget and is available for consultation on executive matters.

In 1955 certain provisions of the 1953 Organic Law concerning the establishment of legislative councils started to come into effect. It would be difficult to visualize these bodies, as at present constituted, offering any threat to the unified will of the régime. However they represent some concession to the opinions and interests of the European residents. In time they may produce seeds of the same kind of effective discontent as were manifested by the French *colon* in Algeria. In essence these bodies act as advisory councils and not legislatures in the American sense of the term.

While each legislative council is a separate juridical creation for its particular province, they all share basic char-

acteristics. Accordingly, it will suffice to describe the structure of one such council, that of the East African province
of Mozambique. This council is composed of sixteen
elected and eight nominated members chosen for a four-
year term. Six members are chosen by various types of
corporate bodies, employers' associations, workers' groups,
cultural and religious institutions, and administrative bodies. One member is elected by Portuguese taxpayers paying more than $350 annually in direct taxes. Only nine
members are chosen directly from electoral districts. Of
the nominated members two must be selected to speak for
the indigenous inhabitants. The electorate represented by
this system are exclusively European either by ethnic origin or by the difficult cultural choice that converts a tribal
African into an *assimilado*.

The second principle, that of "spiritual assimilation,"
adds a distinctive quality to Portuguese rule in Africa. Its
origin may be traced to the missionary zeal that marked
the great era of Portuguese expansion in the fifteenth and
sixteenth centuries. While religious motivation is no longer
dominant, the pattern of behavior that culminated in the
blended culture of Brazil appears deeply rooted in the
Portuguese outlook. Its great merit lies in an absence of
the racial and color prejudice that mars the activities of
other European settlers in Africa. Its weakness lies in the
assumption that the aboriginal inhabitant has only one
possible course before him, a laborious imitation of the
Portuguese model. This attitude justifies unabashed paternalism. African advancement is looked upon as a distant dream dependent upon patient acceptance of an indefinite period of tutelage. The concept that the African
might possess a mind or will of his own that could lead
him to cultural development along non-Portuguese lines is
resolutely barred. From the standpoint of recent Western
experience throughout Asia and Africa, the Portuguese
faith in the irresistible attraction of their culture to African
peoples must be held based on blind provincialism. Spiritual assimilation, when presented as a one-sided demand

to abandon cultural identity in exchange for the beliefs of
another people (which itself has been relegated to a back-
water in the stream of history) invites political tyranny.
To the credit of the Portuguese it may be said that this
notion remains more of a comfortable justification for un-
hampered dominance than a crusade to break down the
basic social coherence of the great majority of the inhabitants.

The third principle, that of administrative differentiation, is the true operative clause of the Portuguese system
of African government. While the Portuguese state is composed of one people, no compelling reasons exist why individuals or groups should possess equality of political,
social, or economic rights. The logic of the Portuguese
constitution permits the two categories of Portuguese citizen and Portuguese native to merge in the transcendental
unity of Portuguese nationality. Each province may be administered separately so that it contributes efficiently in
the manner the central government considers most bene-
ficial to the common culture. Within the provinces, groups
or categories of the inhabitants may be treated on entirely
different terms according to their capacity to forward the
national interest. Thus what might appear as a paradox to
American eyes, equal nationality joined with the grossest
inequality of social rights, lies at the heart of the Portuguese system.

In practice the African tribes are treated as wards of
the Portuguese state. Little is known as to what they receive in the way of education, medical services, public
works. It is certainly less than the Union of South Africa
provides for its Bantu areas and probably less than that
given by any European colonial power with the exception
of Spain, whose possessions are negligible. The frank answer of the Portuguese state is that if its African nationals
seek to better their condition they must bestir themselves
to become civilized. Once this effort has been made the
doors to full fellowship with European compatriots are
thrown open. This attitude is largely theoretical; while the

conditions for becoming *assimilado* do not appear severe
in terms of Western living standards, they lie well beyond
the economic or educational reach of anything but a minor
fraction of the indigenous population. (The term *assimilado* is used to describe a native who has become civilized
in the eyes of the law. All Europeans are accounted "civilized" by virtue of origin; Africans, however, must be able
to read and write Portuguese and have reached a certain
level of schooling before being rewarded with this title.)
Statistics provide reason for skepticism over the progress
of assimilation. Mozambique in 1946 counted 55,451 civilized out of a total population of 5,085,630; by 1950 the
civilized element, which of course includes all Europeans,
had risen to 91,954 of which 4,349 were Negro and 25,149
Colored, while the total population rose to 5,732,767.[11]
Angola boasts larger civilized totals:[12] 91,611 out of a
total population of 3,646,399 in 1946; but the rate of
growth is similar to that of Mozambique: 135,355 civilized, of which 30,089 were Negro, 26,335 Colored, in a
population increased to 4,009, 911 by 1950. Portuguese
Guinea had 8,320 civilized, one-sixth of which were Negro as against 502,457 uncivilized. The plantation economies of Sao Tomé and Principe, created and worked by
African labor imported from elsewhere, show a significant
difference. In 1950 more than two-thirds of the population
—43,391 out of a total of 60,159—were accounted civilized. In turn the civilized element was dominated by
37,950 Negroes and 4,279 Colored against 1,152 Europeans. This seems to indicate that cultural assimilation is
not seriously intended as a goal for the African under tribal
conditions of life; it is only when the indigenous inhabitant
has been uprooted, committing himself wholly to European
standards, that the door to advancement is unlatched. By
an ironical turn of history the Portuguese concept of *assimilado* would seem ideal to meet the economic and social
realities of African progress in the Union of South Africa,
while application of South African dreams of benevolent

separatism would probably improve living standards in
Portuguese Africa.*

Governmental organization of the uncivilized majority is
authoritarian, involving more direct supervision by European administrators than is customary elsewhere in colonial Africa. Juridical principles are laid down by the Statute of the Indigenous Peoples of the Provinces of Guinea,
Angola, and Mozambique. Two of the guiding rules are
that "except when otherwise provided by law, natives are
governed by the usages and customs of their own societies"
(Article 3) and a corollary: "no political rights are granted
to natives in respect of non-indigenous institutions" (Article 23).

Each African province is divided into districts, governed
by district governors; in turn these regions are divided into
primary administrative areas or "circumscriptions" under
an administrator who personally directs indigenous affairs,
presiding over native law courts and the councils of chiefs.
The circumscription is itself composed of administrative
posts, in which junior officers trained in the *Instituto Superior de Estudos Ultramarinos* (Higher Institute for Overseas Studies) at Lisbon are initiated into their careers. A
slightly different system is used if sufficient numbers of
"civilized" are settled in the area. Then the circumscription becomes a *concelho* and the post a parish, with consequent lessening of the arbitrary power of the administrator.

Circumscriptions and posts include tribal groupings
under chieftainships of traditional character. The Portuguese authorities pay these chiefs and exercise strict supervision over their appointment. They are for all practical
purposes instruments of the European administrator. Article 10 of the Statute of Indigenous Peoples states: "the
obedience of the population (to the Chiefs) is the result
of tradition and shall be maintained insofar as the Chiefs

* In August 1961 the Portuguese government granted citizenship to all
its African nationals.

respect the principles and interests of the Administration to the satisfaction of government." No tribal African may leave the territory his Chief rules over without permission from the Portuguese authorities.

It is difficult to estimate how fairly Portuguese administration operates in areas outside the towns and their environs. Opportunities are few for unsupervised visits into the back country by outside political observers. No reports on social, educational, or cultural progress are submitted to the United Nations as Portugal refuses to admit that her African provinces have the status of colonies. In view of Portuguese unwillingness to open these territories to critical inspection or to give the inhabitants access to international bodies to voice complaints it may be assumed that some measure of tryanny, oppression, and corruption lies concealed behind the benevolent phraseology of the various organic laws and statutory provisions.

In this connection the fourth principle, that of economic solidarity, has led to sharp doubts on the part of world opinion. Are the African territories and African peoples being exploited for the benefit of the Portuguese mainland? In the first place it should be observed that the Salazar régime has introduced financial stability into the affairs of the African provinces. A doubt remains, however, as to whether the proceeds of African labor and resources are being fairly distributed between the metropolitan and local communities. Forced labor by Africans for the benefit of private European interests as well as for necessary public works is generally considered prevalent. Article 146 of the constitution of Portugal as spelled out by the Organic Law of Overseas Portugal states that: "The state may compel natives to work only on public works of general interest to the community, on tasks the finished product of which will belong to them, in the execution of judicial sentences of a penal character, or for the discharge of fiscal liabilities." Systems whereby the state supplies or compels native labor to work for private enterprise are prohibited by the Organic Law. However, loopholes in the fundamental

codes still permit administrators, when willing, to conscript
African labor for European use. That this willingness exists
is testified to by a dispatch from the *New York Times* cor-
respondent in Mozambique, published on June 9, 1954.

Forced labor still exists. The Negro in Portuguese Mozambique
is compelled by law to work for an employer six months a year
unless he can obtain a certificate showing that he has put in
the necessary quota of work on his land. Heavy pressure is put
on the district administrators who decide whether a Negro is
to be shipped away to work. Plantations, both large and small,
demand their labor supply as do other employers. The government defends the law which compels Negroes to work six
months a year instead of sitting and watching their wives till
their tribal lands. This law is called an essential element in the
civilizing process, giving responsibilities.

When tax burdens are laid on the tribal African to compel
his labor, the remaining steps needed to direct the nature
of employment are administratively simple. The African
may not move from one area to another without official
permission. A registration card must be carried at all times
and it is forbidden to leave an employer before a contract
period has expired. This allows slight scope for either individual or collective bargaining. It is not unfair to describe the Negro's position as that of personal economic
servitude, tempered by governmental supervision.[13]

As regards landholding (since labor and land constitute
almost the sole capital of African peoples), recent changes
seem to promise greater flexibility and security for indigenous land tenure. The 1955 Organic Law of the Portuguese Overseas Territories set out several principles for
customary land ownership.[14] In the first place, registration
of title is possible, ensuring against seizure or uncompen-
sated expropriation by officials. In the second place, transfer of title becomes possible, though only between natives
and in accordance with tribal usage. Thirdly, title to native land cannot be pledged as security for loans except through governmental organization. Well-advertised
schemes to settle tribal Africans on modernized, coöpera-

tive agricultural settlements have not as yet gone beyond pilot projects. More serious efforts are being made to create immigrant peasant settlements drawn from the Portuguese mainland; the most noteworthy example located at Cela boasts a hydroelectric power development.

Future of the Portuguese System. It may be predicted that the present phase of Portuguese imperialism has arrived at a dead end. Colonial rule by friendly European powers in the lands surrounding Portugal's territories made possible the brutally paternalistic native policy on which exploitation of the provinces was based. Now, anarchic Africanism in the former Belgian Congo, stirrings in Nyasaland, and African self-rule in Tanganyika have breached Portugal's African frontiers beyond hope of defense, at least by her own unaided efforts. On the other hand, liberation of the African inhabitants on the British, French, or Belgian model is by no means inevitable. Salazar's autocratic "New State" could hardly survive the economic loss involved. An alternative exists in a prospect of joining forces with the Afrikaner fanatics of South Africa and the desperate white settlers of the Rhodesias. Though this would degrade the last pretenses of a Portuguese mission of civilization, it might provide a delusion of survival to a doomed oligarchy. Instruments of repression based on the efficiency of Portuguese native administration backed by the armed might of South Africa would in all probability suffice for many decades. However, the decisive factor is how long the international situation will permit the unscrupulous economic exploitation of African labor and resources through the untrammeled dominance of European minorities. Neither Portugal nor South Africa may be considered truly viable power entities in the modern world. Both owe their free existence to membership in a Western bloc of nations. Perhaps the true question at issue is the willingness of the major countries of the West to allow their world position to be imperiled by the dangerous antics of these "hangers-on" of Western civilization. In the case of

Portuguese territories the question is made more acute by the obvious inability of the Portuguese economy to supply either the capital or technological skill to advance the development of natural resources or social standards in terms of present-day needs.

When the artificial peace of Portuguese Africa collapsed in the terror of the Angolan rising of April 1961, Portugal discovered that her colonial policies were condemned even by her allies in the Western world. The shock administered by the United States to the Salazar régime, when on two occasions it joined with Soviet Russia and an overwhelming majority of the United Nations Assembly and Security Council "to deplore the large-scale killings and the severely repressive measures in Angola," has endangered the future of the régime itself. Rebellion carried out in the form of guerrilla warfare supported by the neighboring African states is in all probability a greater strain on the military and economic resources of metropolitan Portugal than that overburdened community is either willing to bear or capable of meeting. Recognition of a Revolutionary Government of Angola in Exile under the leadership of Holden Roberto by the Organisation of African Unity in 1963 placed the united support of independent Africa, with the natural exception of South Africa, behind the Angolan rebellion.

Spanish Guinea. It is tempting to regard the rule of metropolitan Spain over nearly 11,000 square miles and 200,000 African people, wedged between Gabon and Cameroun, as anachronistic. In terms of present-day African nationalism slight reason exists for the perpetuation of unabashed European dominance in this insignificant enclave. On the other hand African nationalism may not be as powerful a movement in its own right as it has appeared in recent days. Without any apparent show of force, Spain holds what it claims to be the two Spanish provinces of Rio Muni and Fernando Po Island in reasonable tranquillity. Politics are barred to both Africans and Europeans alike. Social equality is granted to a small élite of African *emancipados* through a policy of limited assimilation. Three of the six representatives returned from Rio Muni and Fernando Po to the Spanish *Cortes* in 1960 were Africans.[15] Metropolitan paternalism, besides raising standards in health care and elementary education, has guaranteed the system of communal land-holding on which the economic security of tribal and kinship groupings rests. Little evidence exists of internal movements aimed at African unification or liberation beyond a level subject to suppression by the unaided police power of the European contingent. However, the indigenous inhabitants of Rio Muni and Fernando Po will clearly not be left to their own devices by fellow Africans in neighboring territories that have achieved independence. A duel between Spanish paternalism and imported African nationalism appears unavoidable. It is unlikely that this issue will be settled by crude assertion of force on either side. Practical economic and social advances in free border states would, if linked to a lessening of tribal loyalties, prove an irresistible force of attraction. On the other hand, neither African solidarity nor economic progress are inevitable concomitants of independence. Spanish officialdom, safeguarding an orderly and far from intolerable *status quo,* may provide a testing ground, on a small but significant scale, against the spread of African nationalism.

THREE

++++++++++++++++++++++++++++

THE

MULTIRACIAL

STATE

European settlement in East and Central Africa and on the southern tip of the continent is a fact of history. At present it is only in British-held territories in East and Central Africa that the question of making the political state a reflection of a mixed society has been placed, in part, on the shoulders of the local inhabitants. In South Africa, as has been described, government is the instrument of race supremacy, denying the existence of a single society. Elsewhere in tropical Africa metropolitan governments assume almost total authority over the ordering of the multiracial context of the community. The claim of the European settler, and the Asian settler as well, to be counted a true part of the African social structure depends to some extent on his ability to deal directly and responsibly with the indigenous majority in determining group relationships. To achieve this end a measure of political self-determination, particularly for the European and Asian element, is needed. The possibility that any such devolution of power on the part of a metropolitan government may lead to racist rule on the South African model poses one of the major problems of contemporary Africa.

On the other hand, to deny the value of the European and Asian influx into tropical Africa amounts to a repudiation of the major factors permitting technological, economic, medical, and cultural advancement. A balance has to be struck so that the accomplishments of the alien immigrant in producing order out of chaos can be weighed against arrogant claims to perpetual supremacy. African society can only advance or even survive in civilized terms on a mixed basis in many areas. British Central Africa represented a laboratory experiment testing the practicability of having local groups solve this problem on their own account. The demise of the Federation of Rhodesia and Nyasaland spelled the end of a speculative hope on the part of the parliament and people of the United Kingdom that sufficient maturity existed on the political level for a settler-directed policy that would result in a working union of races and interests.

THE FORMER FEDERATION OF RHODESIA AND NYASALAND

The background of the Federation has bearing on the nature of the situation today. In economic terms the three areas—Southern Rhodesia, Northern Rhodesia, and Nyasaland (now Malawi)—are complementary and can only benefit by integration. Southern Rhodesia with the highest concentration of European settlers is the most advanced of the three in secondary industries. The foundations now laid for an iron and steel industry, together with the completion of the $316,000,000 Kariba Gorge hydroelectric power plant on the Zambesi, should provide a major stimulus to industrialization. The famous Copperbelt, stretching along the borders of the Belgian Congo into Northern Rhodesia, acts as the major capital resource of the area. Both of the Rhodesias possess good agricultural land and climatic condition favorable to European-type farming. Predominantly agricultural Nyasaland contributes export crops such as tobacco, tea, and cotton. Approximately 300,000 Europeans can be regarded as permanently settled, largely in Southern Rhodesia, out of a total population of around seven and a half million of which over seven million are Africans.

Historically, the area was in a transitional period of social breakdown when the impact of Western culture was first felt. One hundred years ago Central Africa was inhabited by a variety of tribes living in a near state of war with their neighbors and under constant threat of Arab slave raids from the north. By the end of the nineteenth century what is now British Central Africa had come under British administration, largely through the enterprise of such men as Cecil Rhodes and Harry Johnson working through that adventurous corporation, the British South Africa Company. The different methods by which this was brought about have conditioned to some extent the present social structure in the region. In Northern Rhodesia the British Company extended its sphere of influence peacefully and largely by consent of the ruling chiefs. Accordingly, the continuity of African political organization was maintained by the preservation of the prestige of the chiefs. Southern Rhodesia faced bloodier crises; Lobenguela, an African leader of stature, had to be eliminated, and the crushing of the Matebele and Mashona rebellions destroyed the position and authority of the chiefs. The last proud leader of the older African tradition was a martyr to the new order. Direct administration by white officialdom replaced the indigenous system of rulership. Since the first quarter of the twentieth century efforts have been made to re-create African local government based on the authority of chiefs and their councils.[1]

In 1922 the European settlers in Southern Rhodesia decided by referendum in favor of association with the United Kingdom rather than with South Africa. Consequently, on the expiration of the charter of the British South Africa Company in 1923, they were granted what the British call "responsible government" in a self-governing colony. Even in these days, handing over the fate of millions of Africans to a few thousand Europeans touched the imperial conscience. A proviso was inserted in the constitution of the new colony reserving to the metropolitan government matters dealing with differential (in plain language, oppressive) legislation affecting the indigenous peoples. Still the precedent was made: The European immigrant carried from his homeland not only the right to rule himself but also lordship over the native subjects of the Crown. This decision, not repeated elsewhere in British Africa, has largely determined the situation in Central Africa today. While observing some respected forms of British democracy such as a common roll of voters, the European minority effectively barred the indigenous inhabitants from participation in political or administrative control. The oligarchy of the white became a way of life in Southern Rhodesia.

Northern Rhodesia and Nyasaland, on the other hand, were administered by the Colonial Office in the established British tradition as protectorates of the Crown. In practice this involved as little indigenous participation in the overall control of these territories as in the case of Southern Rhodesia. There was a difference however in the fact that the rulers of the protectorates were trained civil servants serving limited terms overseas rather than interested members of the economic and social hierarchy dominating the life of the community. As a result the welfare of the African, insofar as it could be determined by a product of British public school training, received fair consideration and perhaps even preference over the interests of minority groups.

The decision to create a federal state out of the three disparate colonies was sparked by the European settlers and finally taken with hesitation and considerable disquiet by the mother parliament in London. There is no indication that the indigenous people desired any political amalgamation. Africans in this region lack organs of communal expression, at least in western terms. However, by unusual efforts most of the leading chiefs of the protectorates managed to convey to the British government and parliament their united opposition.

It was the responsibility of the British parliament to ensure that federation did not imply subjecting the indigenous peoples of the protectorates to the unchecked will of the European oligarchy in Southern Rhodesia. Written into the constitution was an elaborate method of appeal from the Federation to the metropolitan government on matters affecting African interests. What was originally planned as a board to stand above partisan politics and later took the form of a standing committee of the federal legislature, received the power to examine all legislative proposals touching on African interests. Such laws as were held detrimental were to be reserved by the governor-general for consideration by the Secretary of State for the Colonies —in practice this meant for final decision by the British government. On the occasion of the first protest by the standing committee concerning legislation deemed discriminatory to the Africans, the United Kingdom government rejected their appeal. Consequently, to the African majority as well as liberal Europeans, this safeguard became illusory.

Fate of the Federation. Rioting in Nyasaland in 1960 embarrassed the United Kingdom government. Use of Southern Rhodesian militia to restore order together with the concoction of a preposterous "murder plot" as an excuse for panicky action by the Nyasaland colonial governor were made subject of criticism by a United Kingdom investigatory body (the Devlin Commission). Subsequent action by the Southern Rhodesian government in declaring a state of emergency in order to curtail still further social and political liberties of the African majority indicated the growth of neo-fascist sentiment among the European community. Britain's Conservative administration committed to a far-seeing though cautious policy of colonial liberation, reacted with comparative firmness through appointment of the Monckton Commission to study and report on the future of the Federation. Published in October 1960, the Monckton Report served as subject of a

London conference between all the governments concerned, with the British government presiding as legal
sovereign.

In 1963 the British government accepted the viewpoint
of African political leaders in Northern Rhodesia and
Nyasaland that the Federation could not be salvaged and
merited dissolution.

Territorial Governments. Southern Rhodesia as a self-
governing colony boasts a governmental system under
almost complete control of its European minority. Theoretically the Southern Rhodesian constitution of 1923,
being an act of the British parliament, is subject to repeal
or amendment by that body at any time. This is not entirely an idle threat; constitutions granting a measure of
self-government have been repealed for cause, as in the
case of British Guiana, within recent times. Discussions
concerning the revision of the Southern Rhodesian constitution initiated by the United Kingdom government
have been held both in London and Salisbury. However,
until substantial changes are effected in the franchise to
permit an African majority some prospect of expressing
its will in political terms, Southern Rhodesia will continue to be governed by a European oligarchy. The internal
distribution of power within such an oligarchy is of slight
interest outside the closed ranks of the power holders. Official policy of this minority European régime, as proclaimed to the world in general, is to lay foundations for
social and economic partnership between the divergent
culture groups in the territory. To a student of government
it would appear that a prerequisite of partnership on the
political level—opportunity to participate in the political
process—has been denied the African majority.

Constitutional structure in Northern Rhodesia and Nyasaland was a direct responsibility of the metropolitan government. Though economic planning and social developments were to some degree surrendered into the hands
of the Federation government, the political organization

of the indigenous inhabitants was not withdrawn from
the Colonial Office. Both territories were ruled by governors, advised by executive and legislative councils in
the established tradition of British colonial government
for backward areas. The first step toward self-government
is invariably marked by the seating of members of the
legislative council by election rather than appointment.
When a majority of the legislative council becomes elective, it is customary for the executive council to approximate a British cabinet, selected from the majority group
in the legislature and entrusted with ministerial responsibilities. This control over the political framework provided
the United Kingdom with decisive leverage in the social
and economic changes sweeping central Africa. Partly as
a result of Prime Minister Macmillan's 1960 African tour,
recognition of the strength of these "winds of change" and
their significance for Western culture as a whole had become a cardinal feature of British policy. Vested privileges
of the European settler, formerly protected by an element
within the metropolitan Conservative party, now tend to
be subordinated to wider policy issues. Thus Nyasaland,
where discontent manifested itself in dangerous rioting,
was placated with progressive constitutional advances in
1960. In July 1964 the new African state of Malawi was
constituted as an independent nation, retaining membership in the Commonwealth.

Constitutional reform in Northern Rhodesia lagged behind that of Nyasaland in 1960 mainly because of the
greater economic interest involved in the Copperbelt. However, the Colonial Office declined to jeopardize the wider
vision of a pro-British East and Central Africa in order
to sustain transitory political dominance on the part of
the fractional European element. Makeshift adaptations
of the franchise to maintain the supremacy of 2.2 percent
of the population—the resident European element—had
become as fantastically complicated as they were blatantly
unfair. In 1961 an African majority was assured in the
Legislative Council as a primary step toward inevitable

self-rule. Full self-government under conditions of universal suffrage preceded the creation of the independent African state of Zambia on October 24, 1964.

Social and Political Issues. The test of a government based not on the consent of the majority but on a future mission to achieve "partnership" between groups at different levels of advantage must, in the last resort, be the use made of political power to lessen economic and social inequalities. The record of the Federation was not encouraging. Before federation, Southern Rhodesia required all native Africans to carry passes when outside tribal areas. African trade unions were denied legal recognition, while penalties of imprisonment or flogging were imposed on Africans who deserted their employment or neglected their duties. By a cruelly misnamed law, the Industrial Conciliation Act of 1945, Africans were effectively barred from certain forms of skilled labor, particularly on the railroads. Humiliating stigmata were permitted to be inflicted on Africans in terms of separate entrances to post offices and banks, exclusion from European hotels and motion picture houses, and separate accommodation in trains, buses, and taxicabs. Little more than token changes in color-bar restrictions took place under federation. Northern Rhodesia legislated against racial discrimination with considerable firmness, distinguishing its social structure even further from that of the Southern Rhodesians. During 1960 the latter colony abandoned even its veneer of British justice by the passage of emergency laws and vagrancy acts that subjected, in practice, all Africans to arbitrary arrest and indefinite detention. Resignation of the Chief Justice of the Federation, Sir Robert Tredgold, in protest against such police state legislation dramatized the issue.

Basic political tensions are related to economic factors which in Southern Rhodesia center in large part on questions of land apportionment. With 48,000,000 acres set aside for 178,000 Europeans and 38,000,000 acres for 2,290,000 Africans,[2] the grievances of an agrarian indigenous population in process of rapid expansion are self-evident. Industrial labor and personal service on the part of the African in Southern Rhodesia is carried out under humiliating conditions—breaches of work contracts, and absences or neglect of duties are treated as criminal offenses in the South African manner. A taint of peonage poisons the employer-employee relationship throughout the colony.

Investment pressures rather than government action can be credited with such progress as has been made to advance the condition of the indigenous labor force. The United States, through some of its more enlightened mining and financial corporations, has played an unusually positive role. The Copperbelt of Northern Rhodesia provides the financial backbone to the economic structure of the whole Federation. While capital from the sterling area is at present predominant, American investment seems essential to maintain and improve an annual inflow of foreign capital of between 75 and 90 million dollars. Speaking perhaps with the authority of some important international corporations behind him, the American consul general to the Federation warned in March 1956 "that the American employer is not accustomed to the color bar and some of its associated problems and that where the distinction exists most American investors will be apprehensive about it as a potential disturbing factor in labor relations. . . . The American investor, however, is going to be slow about investing in a partnership in which he lacks confidence, which he has grounds to fear will break up because of incompatibility of members of the firm." [3]

Recognition of the African mine workers' right to engage in skilled labor probably resulted from the uncompromising stand of the Rhodesian Selection Trust Group, [4] a major operator in this field largely controlled by American finance. The European union of the highest paid mine workers in the world had long enjoyed monopolistic privileges with the tacit consent of their employers and the political administration. In November 1960, negotiations with the Rhodesian Selection Trust and Anglo-American Corporation persuaded the Northern Rhodesia European Mine Workers' Union to end the color bar and make merit henceforth the only criterion for advancement.[5]

Education, sometimes described as the new religion of Black Africa, constitutes an issue of growing political importance. Professor Franck has estimated that in 1958 the education of each African child in Southern Rhodesia received the benefit of less than one-tenth the recurrent and half the capital expenditure made for each European child.[6] This disparity is justified by the European community on the grounds that its contribution to tax revenue on a per capita basis amounts to 15 to 1 as compared to the African contribution. Federation removed control over the educational system from the separate colonial governments, placing it in the hands of the federal authorities. With some justification the African majority suspected that increased educational opportunities, opening up avenues to economic and political advancement, would be denied them for as long as political power remained a monopoly of the European settler element.

Political Parties and Movements. An avowed goal of ethnic "partnership" has not yet resulted in the formation of effective multiracial political parties. European groupings remain the beneficiaries of franchise laws assuring them a practical monopoly of political influence. Personalities, together with transitory responses to a rapidly changing social and economic situation, appear to determine shifting party lines within the European community. The United Federal party won precarious victories for control of both federal and Southern Rhodesian parliaments on a platform of European domination that compromised between the police state of South Africa and acceptance of African participation in political power at some far future date. The Rhodesian Front, successor to the Dominion party, under the leadership of Winston Field, won office in the 1962 elections in Southern Rhodesia. Its avowed objective was immediate independence for Southern Rhodesia under existing conditions of European control. In April 1964 Mr. Field was displaced as Prime Minister by Ian Smith, who represented an even more extremist element advocating secession from all forms of control by the United Kingdom. The status of Southern Rhodesia, debated at the Commonwealth Prime Ministers' Conference of 1964 has become a critical matter of negotiation between the United Kingdom government and the Rhodesian Front regime. A threatened unilateral declaration of independence would disrupt Southern Rhodesia's ties to the Commonwealth and might provoke civil war within the area.

The African majority, largely barred from participation in political rule, has expressed its attitudes through political *movements* rather than parties. Though these movements are clearly part of a general Africanist wave sweeping through Black Africa, they are separately tuned to the charismatic qualities of their respective leadership as well as the particular environmental situation in each colony. Thus the National Democratic party, an outlaw offspring of the banned Southern Rhodesian African National Congress, was later legitimized to represent Africans at the London constitutional conferences of 1960. A rival party, the Zimbabwe African National Union (ZANU) under the leadership of the Reverend N. Sithole, later split African solidarity. The feud between Nkomo, the former leader of a united African opposition, and Sithole has gravely weakened the political position of the African majority. Both parties were subsequently outlawed by the Smith regime.

The "freedom" movement in Northern Rhodesia originated in the African National Congress under the leadership of Harry M. Nkumbula. In 1958 a secessionist group known as the Zambia Congress and later as the United National Independence party successfully challenged the claim of the National Congress to speak for the African majority. Under the dynamic leadership of Kenneth Kaunda, the United National Independence party is projecting social and economic plans for the future of an independent African community in this region. The more narrowly political and economically conservative views of the African National Congress have suffered a temporary eclipse. However, the elements of an African two-party system exist in this region.

African self-government was achieved in Northern Rhodesia in 1962 and was followed by dissolution of the Federation of the Rhodesias and Nyasaland in 1963. Full independence will be granted in October 1964. In the January 1964 elections Kenneth Kaunda's party (UNIP) won 55 out of 75 seats in the Legislative Assembly, Nkumbula's party (ANC) won 10 seats, and a white National Progress party gained 10 seats mainly through a voting device unlikely to be perpetuated after independence.

Nyasaland's Malawi Congress party, conceived among stormy events, displayed understandable tendencies toward militant action. Dr. Hastings K. Banda, clad in the prestige of martyrdom bestowed on him by a fluttery-nerved colonial governor, disciplined his eager followers into a nonviolent opposition.[7] However, the movement remains something more than a political party; through the Youth League, the Women's League, and similar bodies it is conducting a social revolution against tribalism in addition to a political drive toward independence. In 1962 Nyasaland was permitted to withdraw from the Federation and become self-governing. In 1963 Dr. Banda became Prime Minister of a self-governing colony with independence achieved in July, 1964.

All three African movements are controlled, perhaps precariously, by responsible elements seeking to maintain continuity with at least the economic and social advances achieved under colonialism. They cannot, however, afford the luxury of full discussion or the weighing of opposite viewpoints. In this sense they do not approximate political parties in the Western manner; their appeal is to a primary need for social cohesion in face of intolerable conditions requiring drastic change. Freedom—equivalent now to self-respect in the African lexicon—seems worth the sacrifice of certain individual liberties of opinion and action. African movements open a path to group realizations encompassing economic and social upheavals as well as political change. At the best, representative institutions may evolve on the level of one-party systems; alternatively, tyranny may be expected, perhaps cloaked, under racist Africanism or some radical economic ideology.

KENYA

The colony and Protectorate of Kenya achieved independence in December 1963 after seven months of self-government. The number of Europeans, some 65,000, compared to 200,000 Indians and Arabs and 6,000,000 Africans, was an insufficient base for white settler dominance. Nevertheless until recently the European settlers managed to impose a spirited version of minority self-determination on a vacillating parade of governors and secretaries of state for the colonies. A brave statement was made by the Colonial Office in the Devonshire White Paper of 1923:[8] "His Majesty's Government think it necessary definitely to record their considered opinion that the interests of the African natives must be paramount; and that if and when those interests and the interests of the immigrant races should conflict, the former should prevail." This ideal was received uncordially by the Europeans in the 1920's and throughout three subsequent decades. For its part, the British government satisfied itself with enunciations followed by a series of explanations that served as reasons for non-enforcement in what amounted to a continuing state of emergency. In plain fact, the metropolitan government has not been in full control of the situation for several decades. Major factors involved in the impotence of the formal sovereign were the economic strength and social intransigence of the white settlers; "old school tie" bonds between colonial officialdom and the European community; the military importance of

Kenya as a staging base in global strategy; and, in the last analysis, the ignorance of the United Kingdom parliament and its electorate concerning the facts of the situation and their significance in human terms. The end result has been a dizzying spiral of constitutional tinkering, interrupted by bloody revolt and brutal suppression.

The Social Situation. Politics in Kenya are rooted in the harsh facts of physical existence, which throughout East Africa are very harsh indeed for an overwhelming majority of the population. Living conditions before the advent of the European have been described as "a balance between man and his physical environment, enabling the bare survival of the former and preventing serious deterioration of the latter, maintained by a series of epidemics affecting both men and animals, by periodic famine and by intertribal wars and raids." [9] Subsistence living from the soil remains the principal care of the bulk of the people. In such circumstances it is proper to examine economic motivations influencing forms of political behavior. What was at stake to the ignorant cultivator that urged him to challenge a European monopoly of governmental power? The answer in Kenya is land, the right to hold land, to acquire and dispose of it, and finally to use it to grow and market the crops of one's own choice. All of those elemental rights have been imperiled at one time or another by the policies of a government controlled by the European community. In the cautious words of the East African Royal Commission:

The "Highlands" policy and the general tribal approach to land questions adopted in Kenya have introduced a rigidity which has affected the distribution of the population, and has resulted in some people having less land than they could productively use, and some having more. Perhaps more important, however, has been its encouragement of a widespread belief that security in the land can only be ensured on a racial or tribal basis. The circumstances of the early alienations of land to Europeans caused Africans grievances which, despite the subsequent attempts which have been made to put matters right, have col-

oured the whole outlook of a large section of the African population towards land matters. This sense of grievance still persists
and has engendered suspicion regarding all acts of the Europeans and the Government affecting the Africans. . . . Comparatively few Africans have, as yet, been enabled to turn
completely to a full western way of life and this has meant that
these few have, of necessity, been dependent to a large extent
upon being accepted into the community of other races practis-
ing this way of living. That they have not been so accepted is,
we believe, profoundly influencing the East African scene.
These are the new leaders of the Africans, and they are in many
cases embittered men.[10]

Oversimplification of the situation into a struggle between
"black" and "white" for land would miss the point of
Kenya's social tensions. European occupation of choice
areas, particularly the Highlands, was merely one phase of
a deeper problem—that of land reservation on a tribal
basis. Traditional tribal economies with their customary
forms of land tenure simply do not permit efficient utilization of land to meet modern needs. Forms of individual
tenancy and the beginnings of a cash economy must be
substituted for tribal communalism and exclusiveness in
order to feed the people and to save the soil. The responsibility for initiating this process has lain with the British
government. Faced with settler fears and tribal suspicions,
the administration of the Crown took refuge behind the
semijudicial skirts of a procession of investigatory com-
missions. For lack of a true social policy in which all sec-
tions of the community could see their interests reflected
in some equitable proportion, colonial government weakened into the formalities of order, imposed by force over
a sullen sectionalism.

Labor Conditions. Kenya has an African labor force of
around 450,000, almost equally divided between farm or
plantation labor and urban employment. Probably from
40,000 to 60,000 of the urban workers are enrolled in
African trade unions. The policy of the metropolitan government, since the days of the 1945 Labour administra-

tion, has been to encourage the growth of a trade union movement. Though this aim has not been enthusiastically endorsed by local Europeans, no attempts have been made to bar Africans from skilled employment or to enforce economic servitude by legal means as is the case in South Africa. Labor conditions, however, remain a central political question because Europeans and to a lesser extent Asians constitute an employer class monopolizing political power. The facts concerning African labor are candidly set forth in the East Africa Royal Commission Report: "The main relevant facts as regards the African wages problem may be summarized as follows: (a) the general level of wages is low; (b) even where there is minimum wage legislation, as in Kenya, the basis of the statutory minimum has been taken to be the requirements of a single male worker with a very small margin above physical subsistence; (c) the productivity of African labor is generally low; (d) the machinery for collective bargaining is almost non-existent; (e) as a rule there is little difficulty in obtaining ordinary unskilled labor even at the low wage levels which prevail." [11]

From the European point of view, the trade union movement under the able leadership of Tom Mboya became a dangerous political force. In 1952 the legislative council passed a Trade Union Ordinance, giving the government wide powers to refuse or cancel registration of trade unions. In 1955 one of the emergency laws forbade the Kenya Federation of Labor from making political statements on a national basis. From the African viewpoint, European opposition to trade unionism seemed insurmountable as long as Europeans could regulate working conditions by law through their control over city councils and the legislative council.

Education. The approach of an African-controlled government sharpened the disparity between the educational opportunities available for African as compared to European children. Racially integrated schools were accepted in principle in the summer of 1960, leaving the problem of implementation as a future political issue of major consequence. It has been estimated that the present expenditure on African education will have to be increased tenfold if every African child is provided with eight years of primary and secondary schooling. Europeans fear either a catastrophic lowering of school standards or the imposition of a budgetary burden beyond the capacity of the colony to meet.

Constitutional Advances. Mau Mau provided the shock that broke down a European monopoly of high government office. Prolongation of a legal state of emergency over several years permitted constitutional tinkering that retained the substance of political control in European hands despite vague promises of African participation. Neither the Lyttelton Settlement of 1954 nor the Lenox-Boyd Arrangements of 1958 mitigated the growing pressure from the African majority for true advances toward representative self-government. Finally Iain MacLeod, the secretary of state for the colonies chosen by Macmillan to implement a progressive African policy, managed to overcome intransigent settler opposition and African suspicion with some acceptable constitutional proposals. Three major policy aims were dictated by the United Kingdom government as a basis for constitutional development.

(a) Kenya would eventually be independent of United Kingdom control, provided that Africans, as well as other communities in Kenya, took a share in the government of the country;

(b) independence could not take place until the government was responsible to a legislature fully reflecting the differing views of all the people expressed through the medium of a wide franchise;

(c) individuals of every community should have full opportunity to participate in the administration of their country in a spirit of mutual tolerance, though for a time the interests of minorities might have to be secured through constitutional safeguards.[12]

An important innovation in this Kenya constitution was the inclusion of a bill of rights applicable to everyone alike regardless of communal status. This had long been an objective of Tom Mboya and enlightened African leadership, who, with the assistance of Dr. Thurgood Marshall, serving as special adviser at the London conference, submitted a draft bill of rights along American lines for consideration. A perhaps unexpected, though historically correct, insistence on the protection of property rights brought this portion of the constitution into European favor. In the words of the colonial secretary: "Only by this means will it be possible to maintain confidence, and to encourage development and investment, including the attraction of overseas capital, not only in the immediate future but also in the long term." Whether African leaders once firmly ensconced in office will regard this constitutional safeguard as too restrictive of land reapportionment remains to be seen. The final constitution for Kenya before the grant of full independence was implemented by elections in May 1963. Voters elected a central assembly, a senate and seven regional assemblies. The principal issue was whether an independent Kenya should be constituted as a unitary state with a strong central administration, as advocated by Kenyatta and Mboya, or whether a loose federalism should be adopted to placate regional and tribal suspicions of the predominant Kikuyu and Luo peoples. The KANU party won a substantial electoral victory. Its leader, Jomo Kenyatta, as first Prime Minister of a self-governing and later independent Kenya, merited acclaim as "Baba Wa Taifa" (Father of the Nation).

Local Government. Though the central governmental system resisted African participation on a representative basis, some progress was made toward African self-government in local matters. When the British entered Kenya they did not find well-organized tribal groupings under powerful chiefs. Accordingly they have been able to build grassroots political entities without destroying traditional patterns. Headmen, paid from central government funds, were selected to run areas known as "locations," which might or might not coincide with tribal or clan groupings. In 1924 advisory and legislative bodies concerned with raising and spending local funds were created under the name of "local native councils." While membership was generally appointive, consisting of the headmen of locations, provision was included for unofficial members, who were in effect informally elected by village meetings in many areas. By 1950 there were 358 "elected" to 227 nominated members in the local native councils throughout the colony. In the same year they were granted greatly increased powers and their name changed to African district councils. They are now responsible for many important local matters including roads, water supplies, education, public health, agricultural services, and forestry. The central government retains supervisory control with power to dissolve any council or to overrule its by-laws.

Political Parties and Movements. The Mau Mau emergency inhibited for some time the transition of African movements into responsible political parties. However, the presence of elected African members on the Legislative Council in 1960 encouraged the appearance of political parties in the Western sense. African solidarity has not manifested itself in the monolithic form prevalent in Nyasaland or Tanganyika. The Kenya African National Union (KANU) organized along moderately democratic lines is now opposed by the Kenya African Democratic Union (KADU), a merger of five regional groupings. The return of Jomo Kenyatta to political leadership of KANU after his long imprisonment and exile provided a charismatic personality for the organization of African self-government.

European political groupings have divided sharply on the question of the practicality of multiracial parties in a self-governing Kenya. Michael Blundell's New Kenya party advocated moderate policies based on the inevitability of universal suffrage and majority rule sometime in the fore-seeable future. Racist prejudices and fears, however, dominated the outlook of the bulk of European voters judging by results of the 1961 primary elections for communal reserved seats.

The sweeping victory of KANU, under Kenyatta's leadership, in the May 1963 elections resulted in a shift from regionalism to centralism. Over the protests of KADU representatives, many powers of the regional governments, particularly in relation to the police and judiciary, were transferred to the central government.

Kenya's Future. The kind of African state into which Kenya is likely to evolve depends largely on the success of its leaders in resolving tribal jealousies, now that the shadow of white dominance has been removed from the land. Another vital factor is negotiation of a viable East African Federation, embracing Kenya, Tanganyika and Uganda, with prospect of the inclusion of Zanzibar when her time of troubles is over. This development is essential to an economic future, based on an East African Common Market, that would permit sufficient material progress to underpin social and political stability.

ZANZIBAR

A transient example of imperial Britain's skill in nurturing a multiracial society through political means may be found in the spice islands of Zanzibar and Pemba. Zanzibar became a separate Arab sultanate only in 1861, though it had been part of the Arab power area for centuries. In 1890 the then Sultan requested protection from the British Crown, and by 1914 the Colonial Office had assumed effective control. Today, of a population estimated at around 300,000, the dominant Arab element amounts to less than one-fifth, a growing Asian group has approximately 20,000 members, while the bulk of the inhabitants are descended either from the aboriginal Shirazi tribes or from Negro peoples brought to labor on the clove plantations. Political, economic, and religious authority has been concentrated in a patriarchal Islamic system, controlled by an Arab oligarchy.

The primary British objective has been to introduce a measure of economic and social justice into the traditional Arab system. Colonial officials restrained the sultanate from some of the crasser methods formerly employed to exploit African labor. However, it is questionable whether they succeeded in bringing about any substantial rise in African standards of living as compared with those of the Arab landholder or the Indian trader. What was achieved was a systematization of Islamic government along comparatively modern lines. This has had the effect of opening the doors to political power to the oppressed masses, providing a counterbalance to their economic inferiority. As Islam does not recognize racial or color bars, the ruling Arab minority has had to fall back on its economic superiority when faced with a challenge on the political level.

The slow climb toward African participation in government started, in a customary British way, by the formation of local councils. Although the senior commissioner, a British official charged with looking after specific African interests, supervised and controlled the workings of these bodies, they proved a powerful cohesive force in the formation of African opinion. By 1949 the town of Zanzibar had a municipal council composed of nineteen members, of whom four were Africans.

On the central government level, the autocratic authority of the sultan, originally checked by a British resident, was constitutionalized into a Colonial Office pattern of executive and legislative councils. By 1948 an African was seated on the executive council and the Councils Decree of 1956 provided that three members of the executive council should be selected by the legislative council. The government still had an eight to three majority on that former body, over which the British resident and not the sultan presided.

Constitutional provisions implemented in 1961 envisaged a majority of elected members in the Legislative Council together with an unofficial majority in the Executive Council, such a council to consist of a chief minister and four other elected ministers together with three ex-officio members. However, the British resident continued to preside over meetings of the Executive Council. Though Zanzibar was not plagued with problems consequent on European settlement it remained a multicultural society with severe economic cleavages reinforcing ethnic and cultural differences between the African, Arab, and Asian groupings. The achievement of independence in December 1963 unleashed, in a savage revolution, hostilities between the Afro-Shirazi majority and the dominant Arab minority. Deposition of the Sultan and massacre of Arab merchants committed Zanzibar to an unpredictable period of social and political turmoil. Subsequent union with Tanganyika produced a measure of order into a situation that has not yet resolved itself in terms of basic social conflicts.

Political Ferment. The Zanzibar National party under the leadership of Ali Muhsen represented to a considerable extent the age-long domination of the Arab minority over the economic life of the community. Africans, both the indigenous Shirazi tribes and immigrant Swahilis, have only very recently risen above the level of peonage or open slavery.

Two major African-dominated parties, the Afro-Shirazi party and its later rival, the Pemba People's party, concentrated more exclusively on local domestic concerns.

A strong likelihood exists of Zanzibar's becoming a pawn of external forces powerful enough to overwhelm local sentiments or even interests. British colonial rule afforded a brief period of protection against a triangle of world tensions centered on the islands. African nationalism, the

youngest and at present perhaps strongest, would merge
Zanzibar in some regional East African confederation or
even federation dominated by African majorities. Asia's interest in East Africa, long politically ineffective, has become formidable under the banner of Soviet China. Technological aid tied to revolutionary social policies can
be supplied from the East. International politics then,
even more than local issues, will determine whether the
Spice Islands will receive a few more years' grace to grow
into true control of their own affairs. Indecisive elections
held in January 1961 led to what amounted to a tied vote
between the Afro-Shirazi and Zanzibar Nationalist party.
A run-off election scheduled for June 1961 was interrupted
by the first serious outbreak of rioting in the Spice Islands
in the present generation. Social and economic tensions
have apparently mounted to a level that inhibits peaceful
settlements of claims to indigenous political authority on
the part of traditional ethnic and economic groupings. Effective self-government in Zanzibar may have to await the
resolution of wider issues on the mainland that would permit its inhabitants to sink local differences in association
with more viable economic and political entities on a regional basis.

EAST AFRICA COMMON SERVICES ORGANIZATION

A skeleton organization exists for an approach to the economic, social, and even political problems of the multiracial societies of East Africa on a regional basis. In 1948
the question of closer association of the British East African territories was met by the appointment of an East
African High Commission. This body, composed of the
governors of Kenya, Uganda, and Tanganyika, was given
power to regulate a wide range of inter-territorial services,
including railways, postal services, tsetse fly control, and
scientific research on agricultural and health problems. An

East Africa central legislative assembly was then created to exercise legislative control over these service matters.

Wider powers to legislate in general on any matter concerned with the order and good government of the territories could only be exercised with the consent of the executive and legislative councils of each of the territories. Though this shadow of federalism or confederation rested on an extreme voluntary basis, it held out some future promise. Government planning, and even action to meet economic, welfare, or social problems could be referred to a body not directly involved in the racial or tribal tensions of individual territories. At present major achievements lie in the field of research and coördination.

The independent states of Tanganyika and Uganda together with Kenya have continued a planning and administrative structure under the title East Africa Common Services Organization. The Prime Ministers of each of the constituent states comprise the executive. A central legislative assembly is elected by the separate state legislatures from among their own members. A skeleton civil service exists on a continuing basis. International services already in operation under the budgetary control of the Central Assembly provide an excellent nucleus for regional administration based on economic and geographic realities. Skillful use of a central organization of this nature might serve to by-pass some of the more difficult administrative and economic questions involved in any approach to an East African Federation. An East African Common market now accounts for inter-territorial trade equivalent to about one sixth of the external trade of the three participating nations. Fuller economic integration must await solution of perplexing problems of political Federation.

FOUR

++++++++++++++++++++++++++++

TRANSITION

FROM

COLONIAL RULE

Britain's colonial experience has extended over many centuries. Her African territories have reaped the benefits of lessons gained through the nurturing of diverse nationalities within the pragmatic structure of a multiracial commonwealth. India has provided the principal training ground and model for British contact with other racial entities. To repeat the story of India to its successful end, when a new independent nation joins the commonwealth, remains the steadfast objective of British colonial administration. The basic policy was laid down in 1844 by Sir Henry Lawrence, then administrator of the Punjab: "We cannot expect to hold India forever. Let us so conduct ourselves . . . as, when the connection ceases, it may do so not with convulsions but with mutual esteem and affection, and that England may then have in India a noble ally enlightened and brought into the scale of nations under her guidance and fostering care."

For over a century, this disengagement on mutually satisfactory terms has remained a guiding principle, finding fulfillment in the birth of a notable roster of free states—India, Pakistan, Burma, Malaya, Ghana, the Sudan, Nigeria, Sierra Leone, Tanganyika, Uganda, Kenya, Zanzibar, Malawi and Zambia.

THE GOVERNMENT OF UGANDA

The independent state of Uganda was formerly a protectorate of the British Crown. The present situation in Uganda
may be viewed as the consequence of a great many fortui-
tous events, leavened by a slight amount of deliberate policy and considerable good will. A succinct paragraph in
the East African Royal Commission report sketches in the
background:

The main factors which have affected the evolution of the modern Protectorate of Uganda appear to us to have been the highly
organized state of the kingdoms of Buganda and Bunyoro; the
great influence of the Protestant and Roman Catholic missions;
the utilization of Ganda agents to administer other areas, and
the imprinting of the Baganda pattern of administration on those
areas; the agreements which were entered into with the rulers
of Buganda, Ankole, and Toro; the establishment of communications with the outside world by the building of the railway
line; and the absence of the European farmer settler, and the
development of African grown cash crops.[1]

When British explorers and administrators first made contact with the warring peoples of Buganda and Bunyoro,
they found them organized on a political level considerably
in advance of that of other tribal societies in East Africa.
Living under autocratic rulers in communities disciplined
for war and conquest by a bureaucratic hierarchy, they
were advanced in ways recognizable in terms of European
history. To the Victorian empire-builders it was almost like
recapturing part of their own medieval culture. A bemused
admiration for the arrogant Baganda tribe led the British
to support them in the despoiling of the Bunyoro. Further,
they were given firearms to help perpetuate their dominance over other tribal groupings. These policies encouraged the growth of a privileged oligarchy whose vested
interests now stand in the way of national unity.

"The great influence of the Protestant and Roman Catholic missions" is a very polite phrase indeed to describe the transplanting of Europe's religious wars to fertile African soil. These were literal civil wars, in which the converts to the opposing faiths, particularly in Buganda, fought in the villages, in the clans, and in the palace of the Kabaka, paramount chief of the Baganda. Theological differences are no longer disputed with lethal weapons, though political and social organization remains poisoned by bitter sectarian feuds. From the point of view of political stability, the inhabitants of Uganda are paying a heavy price for their introduction into the Christian faith. However, on the credit side, the better part of the education structure of the country may be attributed to missionary efforts.

Uganda is divided into the eastern, western, and northern provinces in addition to the province of Buganda. Partly because a Baganda army under its own chiefs was employed to spread British administration throughout the eastern and northern provinces, the Baganda hierarchy became the agents of political organization. Thus rule on family and kinship lines was replaced by bureaucratic control. Though Ganda agents were withdrawn twenty or thirty years later, a pattern had been established. At one time there were approximately 6,500 salaried chiefs in office throughout Uganda, which made one adult African male in every two hundred a political administrator.[2] The civil service "chief," the end result of this system, is no longer properly linked to the traditional culture he is supposed to represent. Instead he owes place and power to his skill in manipulating a centralized, bureaucratic hierarchy. Tammany Hall politics have become a way of life in a country where representative institutions are not yet fully born.

The agreements made in 1900 and 1901 to define the functions of the native governments of Buganda, Ankole, and Toro and their relation to the protectorate suzerain, have given a federal infra-structure to the emerging state.

Though more than half the population resides in districts outside the agreement areas, political patterns are tailored to preserve the distinctive character of Baganda institutions. The original agreement permitted the Kabaka of Buganda, acting through his council, the great *lukiko,* to make laws for his people that would be valid if not inconsistent with protectorate laws. The governor also held a right of veto. A new agreement, made in 1955 after the return of the Kabaka from exile, widened the autonomy of the regional government. Responsibility was given the Kabaka's government for primary and junior secondary schools, for rural hospitals and dispensaries, and for the agricultural and veterinary field services.[3] The Kabaka's government now consists of six ministries with civil service staff under the general direction of a *Katikiro,* or prime minister. Under British pressure the great *lukiko* has been democratized; 60 out of a total membership of 89 are now elected.

It can hardly be claimed that the present structure of Buganda reflects the will of interests of a "commoner" class. A semifeudal, land-holding group maintains a tight grip over the social and political order. The Baganda oligarchy are naturally reluctant to promote the concept of a unified Uganda, in which they and their privileges would become a minority interest. It was only through forceful action, including the exiling of the Kabaka, that their reluctant consent was won to the attendance of five *lukiko* representatives as members of the Uganda legislative council. Traditionalists in Buganda have resisted direct elections based on universal suffrage. In 1960 with self-government imminent for Uganda as a single political entity the *lukiko* passed a resolution declaring the secession of Uganda from the remainder of the protectorate. Britain ignored this declaration, judging it to be a bargaining move for special consideration of Buganda's claims under the new constitutional arrangements.

Structure of the Central Government. The protectorate government has progressed with comparative smoothness from autocratic colonial rule to representative institutions based on direct elections and universal suffrage. A 1959 committee (the Wild Committee), composed of a majority of Africans with European and Asian minority representation, advocated common-roll elections based on universal adult suffrage to be held in 1961. Problems arising out of the establishment of self-government are less acute in Uganda than, say, in Kenya or Zanzibar with one important exception—the question as to whether Uganda remains a unitary state or assumes a federal character. Two major issues may continue to cause dissension between Buganda and the rest of the nation. Lack of a second chamber in the central legislature to represent traditional tribal rulers denigrates the conservative Bagandan social organization. Again, direct elections to the central Assembly run counter to the existing power system in Buganda which gives the *Kabaka* a virtual right to nominate legislators to the national body. The constitution under which Uganda became independent in 1962 created a quasi-Federal state. The four Bantu kingdoms to the south, among which Buganda is predominant, were granted constitutional guarantees to protect their existing governmental structures. A boundary dispute of long standing between the kingdoms of Buganda and Bunyoro, known as the issue of the "lost counties," was settled in a manner unacceptable to both parties, thus constituting a source of continuing friction within the new state. Lack of clarification of the division of functions between the central government and the Bantu kingdoms remains as a constant threat to national unity.

Local Government. The critical locus of political evolution is to be found in local institutions of government. It is on this level that African participation dominates the decision-making process. In general, British policy has sought to mitigate the bureaucratic authority of a hierarchy of paid chiefs through the development of local councils. The African Local Governments Ordinance of 1949 and the District Administrations (district councils) Ordinance of 1955 to a great extent transformed the chief into an executive officer of a council that held powers of appointment and dismissal. A later law changed the method of selecting and removing chiefs by transferring this power from district councils to independent boards without altering the status of the chief as a local government officer.

The councils themselves form a complicated hierarchy of organizations not yet fully elective. The basic unit is the *muluka* council serving a village or group of villages. In many parts of Uganda, before a system of direct election was adopted, the *muluka* provided the sole direct contact with the ordinary voter. A description of the process in action in the Bukedi district throws light on the almost professional politicking involved. "The taxpayers in each village meet once every three years under the chairmanship of the village chief and elect one person for every 100 taxpayers to sit as a member of the parish (*muluka*) council. Each parish council in turn elects one of its elected members for every 250 taxpayers to sit upon the sub-county council, which in turn selects from among its elected members one representative for every 500 taxpayers to sit on the county council. This indirect system is completed when each county council selects from each 1,000 taxpayers one representative to sit on the district council." [4]

This complicated structure was based on social realities. Communities in Uganda had not yet achieved the degree of union that would permit solution of social questions by voting majorities. Religious, clan, tribal, and family feuds still claimed priority over the idea of a common interest. It is only when social coherence was won on the local level that the next step could be taken toward national consciousness.

Perhaps the views of a former governor, Sir Andrew Cohen, provide the clearest appraisal of the situation.

"When political advances are made either at the center or in local affairs one must not be dismayed when people use their new powers in their own way. Constitutional advance is not a puppet show. A sense of responsibility can only be acquired by exercising responsibility. And in the end, when the constitution of the country has finally to be worked out, the fact that tribal loyalties have been institutionalized may prove a strength, not a weakness. . . . And there are other forces at work in Buganda and elsewhere, forces which are bound to grow stronger in time. These include the broadening influence of education, particularly higher education at Makerere College; the steady growth of a propertied middle class in trade, the cooperative movement, and the professions; the growth of national political parties, not only the Uganda National Congress but the Democratic Party. Although the politically minded have sometimes expressed separatist views in reaction against the Government insistence on unity, in the long run it is difficult to see how they could be in favor of a fragmented county." [5]

Political Issues. As in most largely nonurbanized African communities, the basic interests of the bulk of the inhabitants of Uganda are rooted in the land from which they draw their livelihood. Political realities are determined by questions of land-holding and the disposal of crops. In the words of the East Africa Royal Commission:

A lack of confidence in the secure holding of land is an important circumstance to be taken into account in East Africa. . . . Existing fears are derived from the failure of customary tenure to meet satisfactorily circumstances of land shortage and of demands on land for certain forms of economic use; and from the manner the governments have assumed and exercised legal rights over lands already subject to customary rights. . . . The policy of leaving African land tenure to continue, unguided for the most part, under customary influences has not always led to the individual security demanded by modern economic conditions. In addition, conceptions of "Crown land" and of "Public land" at the will of the state have often, and particularly insofar as the state's powers have been exercised for the purpose of

disposing of land to non-Africans or for what the Africans regard as purposes of non-African profit, given the African a sense
of insecurity in his land holding, notwithstanding the statements
of policy and the complicated administrative machinery designed to reassure him.[6]

The African, as the actual cultivator of the soil, has had
good reason to view with suspicion the casual barterings
between his European overlords and his own customary
rulers at the expense of his means of livelihood. More
often than not, complacent ignorance proved more dangerous to the balance of African society than intentional
greed. The start of the land question in Uganda is a good
example of ill-informed, though in this case fairly fortunate, blundering. The 1900 Agreement with the Kabaka of
Buganda divided ownership of the land of the territory on
the basis of half to the British Crown and the other half
to the Kabaka, county chiefs, and private notables in freehold tenure.[7] The British government's share was waste
and uncultivated land and represented a protective measure rather than a land grab. However, the creation of freehold in land for one particular class destroyed the traditional system of prescriptive right based on clan and feudal
obligations. Though this freehold land, known as *mailo,*
could not be transferred to non-Africans, it created a
strong, prosperous class interested in maintaining the special position of Buganda and its political hierarchy. For-
tunately, it also led to the growth of peasant proprietorship
on a large scale. Protectorate administrations have acted
consistently to safeguard the rights of African tenants on
mailo lands, keeping a watchful eye on cash rents and unfair practices.

Other areas outside Buganda have made claims for similar freehold systems in preference to the type of customary
occupation that makes a cultivator a tenant at the will of
the government. Though customary tenants' rights are
fully protected, an uneasy feeling of political dependency
has remained. Determination of the rules of land tenure
in accordance with tribal customs now lies in the hands

of district councils, so that powerful economic factors have
been introduced into the play of local politics. In 1956
radical proposals were put forward for the grant of individual title in land to African peasant farmers. During
this difficult transition period political movements are likely
to be activated by interests centered in one system or another of land tenure.

No nation-wide political movement has yet manifested
itself in the form of party organization. The Uganda National Congress, oldest of the major political groupings,
has been subject to constant splits and internal feuding. A
Progressive party representing an emerging group of middle-class, educated Africans contends in a minor fashion
with a Democratic party based predominantly on a Catholic religious outlook. Other minor parties reflect traditional
and regional groupings.

In the pre-independence elections of April 1962 a combination of the Kabaka Yekka ("the Kabaka alone") party
based on Buganda and the Uganda People's Congress, a
more national grouping, won over the former ruling group,
the Democratic party, organized around the Catholic influence. Mr. Milton Obote, leader of the Uganda People's
Congress, became the first Prime Minister of an independent Uganda. The economic and social future of Uganda
depends to a considerable extent on the successful formation of an East Africa Federation. However, considerable
opposition to relinquishment of political sovereignty in an
association with the larger states of Kenya and Tanganyika
exists within Ugandan political circles.

TANGANYIKA

As administering authority of the trusteeship agreement of
1946, the government of the United Kingdom accepted
responsibility for establishing eventual self-government in
Tanganyika. The United Nations lacked instrumentalities
capable of carrying out administration on the ground.

Neither the trusteeship council nor its master, the general assembly, was responsible for public order in Tanganyika or any other trust territory. What they could and did contribute is a steady light of world publicity on the behavior of the colonial administrator. That this was valuable can hardly be doubted: though the intentions of a metropolitan government may be excellent, the traditions and background of an overseas service seldom insure government free from arrogance or oppression.

Social Problems. The basic problem of the people centers around the utilization of land. This concentration on economic security is likely to continue until a far higher degree of dependence on an exchange economy and industrialization is achieved. Important, though subsidiary, questions are involved in the fusing of the 120 tribal groups into a social union capable of supporting a nation state and relationships between the close to 9,000,000 Africans, the 21,000 Europeans, and the 100,000 Asians and Arabs.

Land utilization is a political problem in Tanganyika, not because of outstanding conflicts of interest, but through the fact that in African tribal life all social organization revolves around the use of land.

The African's way of life, sense of security, and livelihood are indeed in his view bound up in the land and stock and in the manner in which he uses them. His traditional methods of husbandry have evolved through the centuries as a result of hard experience and trial and error. Memories of famine are always with him, and it is no wonder that he is reluctant to change his way of life unless a better one is demonstrated to him. He knows that if he adopts new ideas and they fail to produce the promised results he will suffer real hardship. . . . A new form of landholding may give better economic results but it may not provide for the varying needs of a family as it grows larger or smaller. Where people are living at a subsistence level there is little or no margin for experiment. Failure may mean not only loss of wealth but starvation.[3]

The original problem stemming from European intrusion lay in alienation of land by the German colonial administration. A total of 1,846,278 acres passed out of native possession, more than half of them into freehold tenure. The United Nations Visiting Mission of 1949 reported that only 6,334,000 acres were under cultivation, by both indigenous and nonindigenous inhabitants.[9] It is probable, however, that out of the total 219 million acres some 40 to 50 million acres are used in some way for growing or grazing. From the governmental point of view the important consideration is whether the Africans fear, even without proper cause, that their access to the land is being imperiled. Petitions made to United Nations Visiting Missions constantly expressed the belief of African groups that the land available to meet the natural increase of their people would soon become insufficient. In point of fact, land shortages appear to stem at least as much from changes in methods of utilization or the rapid deterioration of badly farmed soil as from European occupancy.

Government policy was embodied in the Tanganyika Land Ordinance of 1947, which declared all occupied or unoccupied lands of the territory to be public lands, though the validity of freehold grants and other titles acquired before the passing of the ordinance was protected. Africans individually or in communities lack documentary titles but are held to possess a right of occupancy in accordance with native law and custom. Clumsy enforcement of land utilization schemes has caused bitter hostility among African groups evicted from their traditional holdings. The Meru tribe, for example, suffering from an overdose of bureaucratic stupidity, made spirited appeals to the United Nations Trusteeship Council, winning belated compensation and rectifications from the colonial administration.

Existing European plantations play a key role in the production of sisal, a cash crop of importance to the economy of the territory. The major remaining political problem is how to alter the system of land tenure so that the

African ceases to be a tenant at the whim of any political administration. The first step toward political freedom will be access to the basic means of production without fear or favor from administrative officialdom.

The Chagga success story demonstrates that the problem cannot be solved by easy generalizations. This well-organized tribe, situated on the fertile and well-watered slopes of Kilimanjaro, made an early shift from a subsistence economy to a system based on the cultivation of high-grade coffee. Marketing is in the hands of the Kilimanjaro Co-operative Union, now almost exclusively managed by the Chagga themselves. In consequence a standard of prosperity has been established among the Chagga that well outstrips that of any tribe in the territory. Unfortunately this advance into an exchange economy is based on a one-crop system, particularly liable to violent price fluctuations in the world market. A collapse in coffee prices might find the Chagga without the means to feed themselves. Government must concern itself with such problems in communities just emerging from subsistence levels. Complete divorce of landholding and utilization from political responsibility is too perilous a risk to take with the daily feeding of the population.

Local Government. African participation in the governmental process is a reality in local affairs. Suffrage at this level was traditionally accorded to adult males. The only condition now added is that voters be registered taxpayers. As in other areas, changes in African social arrangements resulting from Western contacts have undermined the authority of chiefs and councils of elders. Tribal and clan communities have themselves evolved compromises between traditional authority and modern institutions. The territorial administration has provided institutional structures elastic enough to permit individual African communities to work out their own problems. The Local Government Ordinance of 1953 allowed for the creation of a pyramid of local councils—parish, subchief, chiefdom, and

district councils. Later legislation made chiefs, to all in-
tents and purposes, executive officers of their councils. As
these councils raise and spend local tax money, they represent the major part of the governmental process comprehensible to the ordinary African cultivator.

The use made of local self-government by the advanced
Chagga people serves as an example of the process. New
influences in Chagga life, the individual prosperity of coffee growers, and the new economic ties provided by their
powerful coöperative union did away with the autocratic
power of the separate hereditary chiefdoms.[10] A modern
conciliar system permitted the emergent élite to be as ade-
quately represented as the traditional element. A further,
and rather surprising, development was the demand of an
up-to-date political organization, the Kilimanjaro Citizens'
Union, for the institution of a paramount chief for the
whole Chagga people. On the surface this might appear a
backward step toward tribalism, but in practice it meant
the control of feudally inclined clan chiefs by the equivalent of a representative monarchy. While this original African solution preserves continuity despite the introduction
of a pattern of representative democracy, it does encourage
local provincialism.

Central Administration. In the 1960-61 session of the
United Nations the British government introduced a resolution to terminate its Trusteeship Agreement for Tanganyika in favor of an independent status on a date to be
agreed upon between the United Kingdom government
and the elected leaders of Tanganyika. This amiable conclusion to colonial domination had been eased by the
previous establishment of "responsible government" under
an African-dominated legislature and executive. The opening up of the franchise to Africans on a common-roll basis,
retaining only qualifications based on literacy or reasonable income (around $200 a year), proved a watershed in
British relations with the peoples of East Africa. In the
judicious words of the London *Times,* "the paternalist

regime that was slowly set in motion under Lord Twining's governorship, based on the principle that political power should be shared equally between all three races, has been rapidly succeeded by acceptance of the principle of political domination by Africans. That this has taken place so smoothly is largely attributable to the moderation shown by the African nationalist politicians. It is tempting to apply the lessons of Tanganyika to its neighboring territories in East and Central Africa." [11] Following the 1960 elections, Julius Nyerere, the architect of racial partnership as well as Tanganyika independence, was ensconced as chief minister, backed by a single-party legislature under his control. Tanganyika became independent in 1961. In 1962 a constitutional change to a Republic was effected while retaining membership in the Commonwealth. Mr. Nyerere, who had previously resigned as Prime Minister, was elected President.

Political Parties and Movements. To the 21,000 Europeans and 100,000 Asians residing among close to 9,000,000 Africans ethnic partnership appears a desirable objective. A monolithic African movement, Tanganyika African National Union (TANU), has met slight opposition in establishing a virtual monopoly over political organization. In fact European and Asian representatives, though not at present permitted to belong to TANU, owe their election to support from that body. Mr. Nyerere has overcome European opposition perhaps too well; as responsible chief of administration he must rely increasingly on trained European personnel, thus leaving himself vulnerable to accusations from his African followers that he has joined the camp of the former rulers. Within African ranks a considerable amount of uncertainty and unrest is denied expression through lack of organized political opposition under a single-party system. Traditionalism, embodied in tribal standards and chiefly rule, is engaged in a deep subsurface struggle against the social revolution concomitant on general education and centralization of economic and political life.

Underlying a political awakening is the hard fact of the poverty or at least underdeveloped condition of Tanganyika's material resources. There is simply insufficient economic means to satisfy basic demands for education, health improvement, and continuous rises in living standards. Politics must obtain these means either from abroad or through close liaison with neighboring African territories. This appears to be the key to Mr. Nyerere's policies. He has judged that the former colonial connection can be transformed by sensible political action into a profitable link with Western finance and technology. "As Tanganyika becomes self-governing we want our growth as a nation to be rapid, our credit to stand high and our independent status to be a beacon of hope to our brothers who are still struggling for justice in other parts of Africa. . . . We have great natural resources. What we must do is to develop these resources ourselves, in cooperation with foreign capital and technical assistance wherever that is necessary; and it will be our policy to attract such assistance and investment from overseas. . . . Our most critical years are going to be the first years of independence. It is during these first years that our need for assistance will be at its most urgent if our economic activity is to start off with a momentum great enough to ensure success in overcoming the poverty, disease and ignorance which is our legacy." [12]

As focus for an East African economic and political confederation, Tanganyika has a promising future. However, obstacles remain grave in terms of reluctance to unite on the part of Kenya and Uganda. A Pan-African movement sufficiently dynamic to overcome local jealousies and different levels of economic advantage might require more extreme leadership than that emanating from the moderate partnership concepts of Nyerere. On the other hand, external backing, particularly in respect to investment and technical aid, might suffice to federate a substantial part of eastern and Central Africa into an important nation committed to Western patterns. A great deal will depend on how the United Kingdom and the United States frame their offers of assistance and coöperation. As Mr. Nyerere observes, "assistance is usually given in order to counter the influence of this or that rival power, or, which amounts to the same thing, in order to buy the friendship of the receiving country provided that 'friendship' includes enmity with the rival. . . . Apart from the politics of foreign aid, there are also the hard economic facts; we know that there are a number of countries today competing for outside investment, and that many of them are in a better position than we are to attract it." [13] Despite some cautious pessimism there is opportunity for profitable and dignified coöperation with African nationalism if political and economic authorities in Britain and the United States realize in time that the Western connection in East Africa is in true jeopardy. Alternatives for economic and social support from Pan-Arabic or Soviet expansionism exist in the face of failure on the part of the West. It is well to remember that in material terms the African has little to lose.

HIGH COMMISSION TERRITORIES

Basutoland, an enclave wholly within South Africa, and the border lands of Bechuanaland and Swaziland hold precarious titles to independent political existence. Where once the interests of the British empire protected them from Boer aggression, now only the conscience of the British people saves them from absorption by an expanding Afrikaner state. On the whole these lands are firmly within the economic orbit of South Africa, though Bechuanaland might exist as a satellite of the Rhodesias. Approximately 70,000 adult males out of a total population of over 500,000 are absent each year from Basutoland, working in mines or on farms in South Africa. A slightly

smaller proportion migrate annually to the Union from
Swaziland and Bechuanaland. Bechuanaland's territorial
account between imports and exports is largely balanced
by remittances from workers across the border. Rail and
road communications are part of the South African system. However, the building of the Bechuanaland section
of the Rhodesian railroad elicited a promise from the British government in 1895 to the effect that the Bechuana
peoples would remain under the rule of the Crown.[14]

Ever since becoming an independent dominion South
Africa has sought to take over administration of these
lands, but the rise to power of the Afrikaner Nationalists
has altered Britain's original intention to cede. Now consent of the inhabitants is held essential to any transfer of
sovereignty. At no time in the foreseeable future is this
consent likely to be forthcoming. South African threats
and pressures, economic and even military, may be inten-
sified in the course of the next few years. It is almost
inconceivable that British public conscience would permit
these African peoples to be surrendered to Afrikaner tyranny.

Structure of Administration. The United Kingdom Colonial Office is now responsible for the administration of
these territories. The high commissioner for the three territories also acts as representative of the British government in South Africa. This dual role keeps administrative
policies in the territories sensitive to the views of South
African politicians. Each territory has a resident commissioner. The social order is not over-complicated by European settlement—Basutoland is for all purposes a native
state and only in Swaziland has land been alienated to
Europeans on any considerable scale.

In Basutoland a well-knit tribal grouping with independent highland traits has provided a valuable substratum for
a governmental structure. The institution of a paramount
chieftaincy holds the people together as an incipient nation. The British administration introduced advisory dis-

trict councils with elected majorities. A central council, advisory to the resident commissioner, served as a transitional stage between the traditional system of nomination by the chiefs and the new elective principle of the district councils. However, in 1960 the Basutoland Council advanced to the status of a full-fledged legislative council with powers to legislate on all matters except defense, external affairs, internal security, and the civil service. These reserved subjects remained within the province of the high commissioner. A shift in favor of popular representation as against chiefly nomination gave a majority for the first time to members elected by District Councils acting as electoral colleges. In order to safeguard the organic structure of Basuto society, substantial powers of nomination (36 out of a council membership of 76) were retained by the paramount chief and senior tribal chiefs. Pre-independence elections are scheduled for 1964 and electoral laws have been altered to create 60 constituencies on a basis of universal suffrage, including the grant of the vote to women. Success of self-government in this economically isolated area is dependent on continuing fiscal support from external sources. A 1960 economic survey mission, for which the British government coöpted Professor Morse of Cornell University as chairman, noted needs for vocational and technical training, agricultural research, improved facilities for the marketing and transport of livestock and agricultural produce, better roads, and aerial and hydrological surveys. Additional United Kingdom aid for Basutoland amounting to $7,000,000 has been added to previous grants and loans approximating $18,000,000 for expenditure within the next 5 years. These subsidies appear of vital moment when contrasted with a revenue and expenditure of around $540,000 raised from indigenous taxation by the Basuto National Treasury in the year 1957-58.

Bechuanaland, lacking any history of tribal coherence, is less advanced than Basutoland in the attainment of political unity. A Legislative Council has now been constituted with limited powers subject both to the veto of the

high commissioner and his right to ensure the passing of
any law he considers necessary. African and white communities are represented in equal numbers on the unofficial majority of the council. Though the Executive Council retains an unofficial majority for the present, its unofficial members are balanced between Europeans and Africans with one Asian member. In 1963 a conference of all
Bechuanaland political parties agreed to request elections
for a Legislative Council based on universal suffrage and
leading to establishment of a self-governing multiracial
state. The British government agreed to holding elections
along these lines in March 1965. Seretse Khama, a chief
once exiled for marrying an Englishwoman, emerged as the
leading figure in this movement toward popular self-government.

Next to Gambia, Swaziland is the smallest of Britain's
African dependencies. Its African population of around
200,000 are of Zulu stock and closely knit under a paramount chief. Early concessions of land have created something of a European problem, but further European land-
holding is now discouraged. This area provides an example of parallel government, with an elected European
advisory council dealing with purely European affairs, and
a paramount chief and a council—consisting of chiefs and
leading men—recognized as the native authority for the
area. Any adult Swazi may take part in discussions held
by the council. The British resident commissioner keeps
in touch through the paramount chief and a standing committee of the council.

Though tribalism remains deeply entrenched, it is of an
enlightened and forward-looking character as is witnessed
by an interview with paramount Chief Sobhuza. "We in
Africa need first support from America in solving our
problems. You people in America are very much interested in foreign affairs and it is your duty to lift up people.
That is a very good step for any civilized man to do, to
give the light to somebody." [15] Tentative movements toward more popular forms of government have been met

by a British proposal to establish a Legislative Council in 1964. The proposed Council was intended to create a legislative body balanced between traditionalist and nationalist African groups. However, Chief Sobhuza created a new political party (the Imbohovodo Party) and won all 24 seats for his alliance of traditionalist Africans and European settlers.

The political as well as the economic future of the High Commission territories must remain, for some time to come, a pawn in a larger struggle between Britain and the Union of South Africa. United Kingdom interests in tropical Africa are now seriously threatened by racist South Africa. Policy clashes involve the immediate future of the Rhodesias and perhaps even the whole east coast of the subcontinent. A useful asset on the British side is the possession of enclaves of African self-government in the heartland of the Union. On the other hand, South Africa may retaliate with a virtual economic blockade against the marginal livelihood of the inhabitants of these territories. Neither Britain nor South Africa is likely to make open declaration of its intentions. The struggle being waged around the High Commission territories serves as reminder that the future of tropical Africa still remains for a large part in the hands of metropolitan powers with established patterns of control. Distant rumblings from African nationalism, the United Nations, the United States, or the Soviet powers do not serve to remove responsibilities at present resting on British officialdom to face and counter expansionist ambitions on the part of South African racism.

SIERRA LEONE

This West African community, with a population of about 2,260,000, presents problems of political organization that foreshadow some of the difficulties many emerging African states are likely to encounter. White settlement has not resulted in a conflict of interests between Europeans and natives; the principal obstacles to the achievement of self-government lie in the tensions within the African community itself.

Originally founded as a settlement for freed slaves in the closing years of the eighteenth century, Freetown became the home of a hereditary African and mulatto middle class calling themselves Creoles or, sometimes, Sierra Leoneans. Constitutional structure followed the social pattern; Freetown and the coastal strip became a Crown colony, the tribal backcountry a protectorate. Establishing economic and cultural bonds between the educated and tribal groups and encouraging the Creole middle class to provide leadership for the whole community is here the major prerequisite to self-government.

The independence of Ghana has encouraged an increased sense of responsibility among West African peoples and politicians. Social feuding behind the comfortable skirts of British colonial rule has become disreputable. Yet tensions between tribal patterns and those of educated individualism remain a source of resentments readily translated into political issues. The Freetown riots of 1955 and later disturbances in the protectorate indicated a critical stage in social development. It is probable that tribal youths migrating into Freetown sought to assimilate themselves to middle-class standards and that resentment was sparked by efforts of conservative Creoles to guard their culture as a matter of hereditary right. The report of a commission of enquiry into disorders in the protectorate found that grave local maladministration arose from corruption and extortionate practices on the part of chiefdom authorities.[16] Autocratic traditional systems had evidently been outgrown, and a purge of chiefs was followed by the establishment of district councils directly elected by the taxpayers.

Central Governmental Structure. The colony and protectorate shared the same institutions of central government.

Recent constitutional arrangements, particularly with regard to electoral reform, were conceived by a five-man African commission under the chairmanship of an English constitutional scholar. Universal suffrage was declared a goal attainable by 1961 and single member constituencies were made the rule throughout the territory.

Political Parties and Issues. Political parties in Sierra Leone still reflect something of the split between colony and protectorate. The Sierra Leone People's party, led by Sir Milton Margai,° draws its main support from the protectorate. Since its formation in 1951 it has been the majority party in the legislature, winning 26 of the 39 seats open for direct election in 1957. It has also gained support among the indirectly elected paramount chiefs and from independents. In April 1961 Sierra Leone achieved independence as a unitary state. Sir Milton Margai and his SLPP party assumed control of the government. In the 1962 elections, the first held under universal suffrage, an opposition party, the All Peoples Congress led by Siaka Stevens, made considerable inroads on the government majority.

True independence means financial independence and this may present difficulties. Though Sierra Leone is principally an agricultural country, much of its wealth is derived from mineral production and export, particularly from diamonds and iron ore; government finance relies heavily on the Sierra Leone Development Company Ltd., a British enterprise founded in 1930 to work the iron ore deposits. Sierra Leone's financial viability may well turn on the measure of success achieved by the government in their present endeavors to check the trade in illicit diamonds—revenue from diamond exports might be increased as much as a fourth to around $6,000,000. In the meantime the United Kingdom government has offered, and Sierra Leone accepted, assistance in the form of loans,

---

° In 1964 Sir Milton Margai died and was succeeded in office by his brother Albert Margai.

grants, and technical assistance to the extent of around $21,000,000. Economic expansion, defense, and the costs of transition will accordingly rest in large part on the shoulders of the metropolitan power. To some degree then, political independence will be curbed by continuing economic dependency.

THE COLONY AND PROTECTORATE OF GAMBIA

The obligation to become a self-governing nation imposed by Britain on all of her colonies that do not rank as strategic bases weighs somewhat heavily on a riverian strip some 300 miles long and 12 miles across, wedged into the heart of Senegal. As in Sierra Leone the inhabitants lack a common cultural experience. Bathurst, with the status and history of a colony, is separated from the tribal societies of the protectorate. In 1963 Gambia achieved internal self-government under a ministerial system. Foreign affairs, defense and internal security (a most important limitation), however, remained responsibilities of the British Governor. In the colony Bathurst has a democratically elected Town Council and Kambo a Rural Authority. The inhabitants of the protectorate are less advanced in exercising effective control of their own affairs under conditions of popular government. There are four divisions in the protectorate, each division containing a number of districts under the rule of a head chief. A Native Authority and Native Tribunal is established for each district. From a realistic point of view, particularly in the light of happenings in the former Belgian Congo, it is probable that the political unity of the territory is underwritten by the Gambia Police Force distributed throughout the colony and territory. This small but efficient body has become increasingly Africanized in its higher ranks. Of the seven top officers two are now African and the personnel of other ranks including chief inspectors is wholly African. A disciplined tool is accordingly at hand for government of the country by an indigenous régime when sufficient social unity is achieved. Constitutional talks with the British government in 1964 foreshadowed independence in February 1965. Prime Minister Jawara of Gambia negotiated a Defense and Foreign Representation Agreement with Senegal to take effect on Gambian independence, placing Gambia under Senegalese protection at least in relation to external affairs.

The economics of a bare livelihood constitutes the principal issue in Gambian affairs. A British understatement points up the realities: "The Gambia has few natural resources and in consequence its financial position is often not happy." [17] Ninety percent of the inhabitants are peasant farmers with ground nuts as their main cash crop. In order to keep the economy stable, the price the African peasant receives for his groundnut crop has been fixed with the aid of a subsidy from the British government.

FIVE

++++++++++++++++++++++++++++

INDEPENDENT STATES—

ENGLISH-SPEAKING

Terms such as nationhood and independence, born of Western historical experience, should be used with caution in African surroundings. Independence is a relative term in tropical Africa. Although self-government, with its absence of alien ascendancy, seems essential for equality of status with other peoples, this does not preclude realities of economic and technological dependence. Inferiority and frustration can be imposed on tropical Africa by neglect as well as by dominance. The modern world is a network of interlocking agencies of production, distribution, and communication of material and cultural values. If the history of a people has not won it a place in this system, admission lies at the grace of the technologically fortunate. In sub-Sahara Africa, coöperative relationships with wealthier communities have to take precedence over separatist tendencies for some time to come.

When comparing the fortunes of Ghana to that of his own country, the Liberian ambassador to the United States pointed out that "the United States did not care about a colony on the coast of Africa and we were left alone and struggling, to vegetate in the midst of developing European colonies. . . . By contrast the liberal colonial policy of Britain was to extend great efforts to develop her colonial holdings and build them up materially." [1] It is not necessary to invent a mystique of ethnic or cultural divergence to explain why tropical African states are likely to vary from European patterns. They cannot afford the self-centeredness that marked the pioneers of the Industrial Revolution. In order to survive in the growing scramble for use of the world's resources, African political forms must be bent to the shape of economic necessities.

LIBERIA

It is tempting to moralize over other peoples' histories. Liberia, partly because of the fine phrase in her constitution of 1847 stating an objective "to provide a home for the dispersed and oppressed Children of Africa," lies open to invidious comparison between intent and achievement. Without reciting scandals in her century of political independence, episodes of slavery and forced labor, financial skulduggery requiring international correction, it may be questioned whether the right to the title of "free African nation" has been established. The Liberian state appears to have been, and to a large extent still is, a proprietary affair involving ownership of the government apparatus by a hereditary caste of around 15,000 descendants of Afro-Americans. Whether the 1.5 million indigenous tribesmen approve of the political state run from Monrovia or how many of them can even speak or understand its official language is not yet known after a century of rule.

Constitutional forms were imported from the United States. The adoption, however, of a Presidential type of government with a legislature divided into a house of representatives and a senate, did not ensure constitutional government along American lines. Checks and balances, either legislative or judicial, on the personal authority of the president are virtually nonexistent. The representative principle in terms of majority participation in the governmental process has hardly advanced beyond eighteenth-century standards. The senate is composed of ten members representing five coastal counties dominated by the Monrovian oligarchy. The house of representatives has 31 members of whom only three are chosen by the hinterland population. A classification of civilized or uncivilized, based on an understanding of the English language, is used as a criterion for suffrage rights. Sixty thousand of the indigenous inhabitants now qualify to vote for their three representatives.

For over 80 years a one-party system has held sway, based on the dominance of the True Whig party. The present chief executive, W. V. S. Tubman, remains in office as the beneficiary of a constitutional amendment ratified by the gratifying figure of 155,792 votes out of a total of 155,792 votes cast. In 1959 and 1963 President Tubman was re-elected to office in landslide victories. He has broken tradition by introducing persons of tribal descent into high office. His reputation at home and abroad is that of an energetic administrator and advocate of social welfare. Unfortunately the long tradition of personal rule, combined with the oligarchic monopoly of political benefices, denies the president a reliable administrative machine to carry out his policies. The practice of demanding "cash" for any kind of service or favor is so widespread as to make graft a major order of government business on the lower levels of administration.[2] The government has failed to achieve standards of health or education comparable to those prevalent in Ghana or other West African states.

Inefficiency, corruption, autocracy, and even caste rule might be tolerable under transitional African conditions if satisfactory links were forged with feeling and aspirations for the future held by the bulk of the inhabitants. Neither in Nigeria nor in Ghana do dominant administrative machines follow strict Western codes of political ethics, but they can boast with truth that they hold the loyalty of inarticulate majorities. This is not the case in Liberia where the rhetoric of the president and the ruling oligarchy are addressed principally to Western ears.

Two French observers described Liberia recently with perhaps more wit than justice as *"esclave et enclave du dollar.*" [3] It is probably more accurate to charge the United States with the consequence of her neglect than to reproach her for sporadic intervention in Liberian affairs.

Raymond Leslie Buell has provided a classic analysis of United States policy in Liberia to the year 1928 and there appears little need to reëvaluate his conclusions.[4] Briefly, the private effort of the American Colonization Society to establish a government of immigrant Negro Americans over the back country tribes (1816-42) received scant governmental attention from Washington until the British challenged the nature of American interests in 1843. Then the American secretary of state replied in equivocal terms: ". . . this Government regards it [Liberia] as occupying a peculiar position and as possessing peculiar claims to the friendly consideration of all Christian powers; that this Government will be, at all times, prepared to interpose its good offices to prevent any encroachment by the colony upon any just rights of any nation; and that it would be very unwilling to see it despoiled of its territory rightfully acquired, or improperly restrained in the exercise of its necessary rights and powers as an independent settlement." [5] When in 1847 the American Colonization Society relinquished their political control in favor of an American-styled constitution, Britain almost immediately recognized the new government but the United States delayed recognition until 1862.

The ability of the government at Monrovia to maintain control over the tribal majority in the back country remained questionable through the first decade of the twentieth century. In 1915 the Kru peoples fought for their freedom, or at least a preference, to place themselves under British control. The Liberian Frontier Force was incapable of mastering the revolt and an appeal was made to the United States government. After pledges had been received for reform of tribal administration, the U.S.S. *Chester* was dispatched with modern weapons for the Liberian Frontier Force. The result was near decimation of the Kru tribe. American policy unquestionably enabled

the Monrovian élite, descended from the original immigrant freedmen, to remain the effective government. It
would be unfair, however, to regard these American-Li-
berians as an exclusive caste; they intermingled with the
indigenous inhabitants, representing, eventually, educational and cultural standards brought from the United
States rather than a blood group.

Until comparatively recent times Liberian finance has
remained in a condition of chronic anarchy. United States
intervention in this area formed the crux of American-
Liberian relations. A loan of $1,700,000 through American
banks was negotiated in 1912, following on a report of a
commission sent to Liberia in 1909 by Elihu Root. Though
an American receiver general of customs, who also acted
as financial adviser to the Liberian government, was appointed to safeguard the loan, an attempt was made to
give the transaction an international aspect through the
addition of British, French, and German subordinates. In
1914 total American control became necessary when
Europe went to war. Subsequent efforts in the twenties to
obtain supplementary loans collapsed in the face of increasingly rigid American demands, which included control of the Frontier Force, native administration, and the
virtual subordination of the Monrovian government to a
highly paid American team. The pattern of American relations had relapsed into the politico-financial imperialism
current in the Caribbean area at that time.

The Firestone Agreement of 1926 constituted an important departure in American-African relations. In terms of
material advancement, the entry of the Firestone Company
into Liberia may be viewed as having brought substantial
benefits to the economy and social organization of the republic. It is another matter whether the governmental policy inaugurated by these transactions created sound pre-
cedents for the future development of American-African
relations. The concept of the Open Door—weakened by
the concession system adopted by European powers—was
virtually abandoned when the United States government

became to a great extent the agent of a private concessionaire.

Firestone entered into two agreements, one concerning
the terms on which it received its extensive plantations and
the other for a loan of $5,000,000 to the Liberian govern-
ment made by the Finance Corporation of America, a
subsidiary of the Firestone Company. The loan agreement
required supervision of both customs and internal revenue
by a financial adviser designated by the president of the
United States, though officially appointed by the president
of Liberia. This in effect placed the United States government in the position of a collector, manipulating the reve-
nues and social policy of a foreign country in the interests
of a private corporation. A contemporary criticism of this
procedure by Dr. Buell remains prophetically valid.

"The American Government is related to the Loan Agreement
to the extent that the President of the United States designates
the Financial Adviser to the Liberian Government, and recom-
mends the military officers to be appointed to the Frontier
Force, and that the Financial Adviser informs (and presumably
consults with) the State Department in regard to the appointment of other Americans who control the financial activities of
the Liberian Government. Moreover, the State Department under certain contingencies arranges the arbitration of disputes
under both Firestone and Loan Agreements. As a result of these
agreements the State Department, unless it departs radically
from the policy which it follows in Latin America and China,
will defend American capital and American control over Liberia
against British, French or German aggression. . . . The activity of the Departments of State and Commerce in promoting, in
the midst of this secrecy, American enterprise in Liberia, and
the disregard and lack of knowledge of the American Government of the effect of the entrance of such enterprise upon the
people and Government of Liberia is disconcerting not only because of this particular instance but because it is symptomatic
of what may happen on a larger scale in the future. America
has become the reservoir for the capital of the world. . . . It
is important that the United States, the people of which do not
wish to be associated in a territorial scramble or in the abusive
exploitation of primitive peoples, should work out methods to

direct foreign investments along intelligent and socially benefi-
cial lines." [6]

Partly because of its sponsorship of the Finance Corporation, the United States missed a unique opportunity to
implement its long-term objective of international supervision over the affairs of Black Africa. By 1929 the scandal
of forced labor, slavery, and ill treatment of the Kru peoples had reached a point where the League of Nations
created a Commission of Enquiry consisting of representatives from the United States and Liberia under the chairmanship of a League official. Reforms were promised by
the Liberian government in return for financial assistance
to be arranged by the League. A Liberian committee was
then appointed by the League and the United States
agreed to serve as a member, indicating an apparent willingness to compromise its special position under the Loan
Agreement. The resulting League Plan for Assistance included the nomination of foreign commissioners to be responsible for public peace and order throughout the whole
country, and the appointment of foreign affairs, all under
the control of a chief adviser appointed by the Council of
the League. In some respects this plan foreshadowed the
1960 intervention of the United Nations in the Congo. The
Liberian government accepted as a means of escape from
its financial morass. However, the Finance Corporation ob-
jected and, receiving backing from the United States administration, successfully blocked implementation of the
plan. A Foreign Policy Association Report of 1934 criticizes
American policy in the following terms. "If the American
government had wholeheartedly supported the first League
plan, the Finance Corporation, which had no sovereign
rights, could not have blocked the League's terms for its
assistance to Liberia. But the League could not carry forward its scheme against the opposition of the United
States. Under such circumstances, the League had to
choose between ceasing its efforts on behalf of Liberia
and revising its plan to suit the United States and the

Finance Corporation. . . . One result of this deadlock is that Liberia has escaped any form of responsible foreign control." [7]

Liberia subsequently proclaimed a moratorium on the Finance Corporation loan and further efforts to provide international assistance through the League ended in failure. In 1934 the British representative at the League proposed the expulsion of Liberia on grounds of gross misconduct and irresponsibility. At the same time the British government instructed its ambassador at Washington to convey the following message to the American Secretary of State: "His Majesty's Government are aware of the deep interest which the United States Government have always taken in the fortunes of that State, which indeed owes its foundation to American enterprise and philanthropy. On the material side Liberia is rendered dependent upon the United States Government by the extent to which her financial machinery is already in American hands and organized in conformity with a contract entered into between the Liberian Government and an American Corporation. . . . His Majesty's Government are ready to cooperate to the utmost of their power in any well-considered measures which the United States Government may consider appropriate to the occasion." [8] Resisting British pressure to proclaim a protectorate over Liberia the United States chose to permit the republic's economy and social progress to stagnate for a decade.

Entry of United States into World War II instigated an assertion of specific American claims in Liberia which ran counter to traditional policies of the United States toward Africa. Neutralization of African lands was forgotten, while the American government sharply prodded Liberia into a declaration of war against Germany. The leasing of the Roberts Air Field Base in 1942 brought with it a gift of a road-building program of significant value. Approximately $22,000,000 was expended on improving the harbor at Monrovia. In 1945 the Export-Import Bank granted a loan of $45,000,000 for loan construction. A five year plan for economic and social development was inaugurated in 1951 at the cost of $32,500,000 and in 1953 was extended into a Nine-Year Development Program.[9]

Liberia may now be described as a comfortable American economic preserve, an enclave if not the slave of the dollar. Another great concession was granted in 1949 to the Liberian Mining Corporation, sponsored by the Republic Steel Corporation and the Export-Import Bank. The Bank of Monrovia, which serves as a depository for the government of Liberia, is owned by the First National City Bank of New York.[10] Perhaps this policy of exclusive American development is more practical and of greater immediate benefit to the inhabitants than more idealistic concepts of free trade, international coöperation, and African neutralization. On the other hand future American policy toward Africa may be compromised by a privileged position in Liberia. American interests have been identified with that of a régime, one constituted on a very narrow base and far from invulnerable to the gusts of nationalistic emotion shaking its neighbors. Conceivably the experience of Cuba may be repeated with disastrous consequences to the United States' present and future standing throughout the whole of Black Africa. Though immediate indications remain bright, the American position in Liberia stands in contradiction to wider policy aims for Africa as a whole. The character of an exclusive concessionaire is a difficult one to sustain amid the turbulent unfolding of African nationalism.

NIGERIA

The crucible in which the lasting shape of African statehood will be forged is more likely to be Nigeria than Ghana, Liberia, or French Black Africa. In size, resources, and population Nigeria possesses the attributes required to constitute a viable nation state. Her 55,653,000 inhabitants have had fifty years' experience of living together under common rule. The basic apparatus of administration, police, civil service, and communications has been constructed on a single pattern using mostly Nigerian personnel. Hope of economic development depends almost entirely on the establishment of social and political unity. The British suzerain sponsored national independence and no enemies threaten the emergent state on its borders. In consequence Nigeria is free to pioneer in a search for workable solutions to the African situation. She may carry the good will of the Western world with her on this adventure, but the inescapable facts of African tradition and organization will not yield wholly to borrowed patterns. A Nigerian solution to the question of political unity must be forthcoming before the rest of tropical Africa can safely embark on the final road to independence. What remains to be solved is the willingness of the people to coalesce into a nation. At present, loyalties and interests are concentrated at the regional, tribal, and village level. Emotional and pragmatic incentives have to be created by political movements to beguile the community into wider social patterns.

The Federal Structure. The component parts of the federation are the coastal town and colony of Lagos, bustling and sophisticated; the northern region, containing over half the population, Islamic and still largely feudal; the eastern region dominated by the intelligent, well-organized, and somewhat aggressive Ibo peoples; the western region with its historic memories of great kingdoms ruled by the Obas of the Yoruba clans; and a small mid-west state carved out of the western region in August 1963 for mixed reasons of geographic convenience and political expediency. The differences separating these communities from one another are easily exaggerated. In essence they all are African peoples, sharing a period of rapid transition that affects both social ties and means of livelihood. Time, economic change, and growth of communications are working on the side of integration. Ambitious, well-educated, far seeing individuals in every region are attracted to the service of the new state. The only real obstacles in the way of wider political horizons are inertia, suspicion, and sloth. An institutional framework that maintains the appearance of regional self-government while bringing the leaders of each area to work together in a central government is probably the most effective political instrument that can be achieved under present conditions.

The sovereignty and independence assumed by the Nigerian nation on October 1, 1960, carries with it responsibilities, to its own people and to West Africa as a whole, that outweigh the pursuit of regional advantage. With the advent of true self-government administrative competence in Nigeria remains a scarce commodity monopolized to a large extent by an educated élite. The position occupied by this key personnel bears some analogy to the *novi homines* (new men) who led Tudor England from feudal society into modern times. Faced with the need of national unity among tribal groupings, the new administrative class tends toward an anti-traditional bias. A strong federal system appears to be the minimum level of political cohesion acceptable. The goal of "a more perfect Union" may readily be borrowed from American history as the immediate objective of an emergent Nigeria.

Constitutional Developments. A constitution drafted for independence in conjunction with the British Colonial Office and sanctioned by the British parliament obviously represents a transitional stage in Nigerian constitutional development. However, the pattern appears stabilized in a mold blending a British model of federal government as practiced by the commonwealth of Australia with the exemplar of the United States. The parliament of Nigeria is elected in single-member constituencies on a population basis of approximately 1 member for each 100,000 people. It consists of a house of representatives and a senate. The latter body has revisionary rather than primary powers; its present composition of 36 senators, 12 from each region, gives it something of the conciliar character intended for the original Senate of the United States. In addition an early American experience is repeated in the nomination of senators by the regional governments subject to the approval of their legislatures. Executive power resides in a council of ministers who constitute a cabinet form of government under a prime minister responsible to parliament. The judiciary and civil service function outside partisan politics in the strict British tradition. African conditions have dictated a variation of both British and American customs with regard to control of a central police force by a police service commission outside the scope of partisan politics. This commission consists of two members chosen by the government in power, two members chosen by the chief justice of the federation, and a chairman selected by the governor-general at his own discretion. For some critical years the viability of the federation may depend on the continuance of a central police force aloof from the type of regional jealousies and demagogic passions that wrecked the independence of the Belgian Congo.

Britain's useful device of a head of state's acting as the repository of legal and constitutional powers though politically inactive has been followed, for the time being, by the continuance of the office of governor-general. Dr. Azikwe's selection as first governor-general of an independent Nigeria inaugurated the office as a symbol of national unity. This fiery politician has claims to the title of father of Nigerian independence and unity. His acceptance of nonpartisan office dramatized to the country the dignity of nationhood and the importance of unity.

Division of functions between federal and regional governments may prove delicate at the outset. However, as has happened in Australian and American federal developments, constitutional arrangements are likely to adapt themselves to realities of social and economic integration. The immediate temptation is not the trespassing by central or regional governments on each other's juridical preserves; a graver danger lies in attempted seizures by political movements of the true instruments of power left by the British—the trained civil service and well-disciplined Nigerian Police Force. If, with the help of informed public backing, the constitution proves strong enough to keep these powerful instrumentalities out of irresponsible hands, the wisdom of the judiciary may combine with normal political processes to settle a division of powers to meet changing needs.

Regional and Local Government. The constitutional pattern of regional government is gradually assuming a similar form. Regional legislatures are all now bicameral, each consisting of a house of assembly and a house of chiefs. Each region has an Executive Council of Ministers headed by a premier, who is normally the leader of the majority party in the Assembly. After 1954 the American concept of federalism was substituted for a prevailing Canadian concept: in place of the regions being limited to lawmaking on specific subjects, they were granted residual and concurrent powers with the central government being confined within the boundaries of enumerated powers.

Regional governments have been made possible and their character is still determined by an infra structure of local authorities. Lord Lugard's policy of "indirect rule" elevated indigenous structures of authority to an important place in the general government of the country. To some extent this policy protected traditional rule against healthy winds of change, particularly in the northern emirates. In eastern and western areas, however, a fairly rapid evolution has brought the original Native Authorities, based on the powers of chiefs or headmen, into line with democratic western institutions. A local franchise based on universal adult suffrage is envisaged in the Eastern Region where provincial assemblies are planned as a further step toward democratic decentralization. In the Western Region, divisional district and local councils, though accepting the principle of an elected majority, provide for the appointment of traditional members up to one quarter of the council membership. The Northern Region has lagged behind the rest of the country in bringing democratic methods of government down to the local level. This reflects a difficult transition from the authoritarian rule of the feudal emirs to the administrative control of the new educated élite. A start has been made in the establishment of Provincial Councils with elected members and Native Authority Committees to coördinate the work of the traditional Native Authorities. An official from the regional government joins in the work of these committees.

Minorities. One of the major unresolved questions in the political future of Nigeria is that of the right of minorities to form their own political groupings. Dissatisfied ethnic, linguistic, or cultural groups are likely to impose the type of strain on budding representative systems that modern India has experienced. Political movements created to win independence have tended to evade the true complexities of Nigerian society. Generalizations such as the division of Nigeria between the Hausa-Fulani culture, the Yoruba peoples, and the Ibo societies endangers the cultural and political rights of many people who do not fall within any of these groupings. The success of the major entities in winning recognition for their claims has encouraged minority bodies to demand the status of new regions or provinces for their own specialized cultures. Following the report by the constitutional conference of 1957, a nonpartisan commission of enquiry was given the following terms of reference for a study of the problem:

Though the desire for the creation of new States in part arises from the fears of minorities it would be impracticable to meet all these fears by the creation of new States. There are many different ethnic groups and peoples in Nigeria and however many States were created, minorities would still inevitably remain. It would therefore be the task of the Commission to propose other means of allaying these fears and to consider what safeguards should be included for this purpose in the constitution.

During the next decade political leadership in Nigeria will have to turn from the task of winning independence to the reconciliation of conflicting interests at home. This will present difficulties, as extremism and intolerance are frequently bred in the exciting atmosphere of a struggle for independence. Existing political parties may find it hard to renounce tribal origins and connections in order to provide true representation for minorities within a united Nigeria.

Political Parties. Party organization in Nigeria is in the process of completing a spiral cycle of development from its origins in a national liberation movement through a phase of regional and tribal groupings to renewed national standards in terms of true political parties. Dr. Azikwe's political career illustrates this process. Starting as the fiery leader of Nigerian liberation from colonialism, "Zik," led a Nigerian Youth Movement originally intended to blanket the whole country. Resistance from the Western and Northern regions to Ibo leadership in political and social ideas led to the creation of the National Council for Nigeria and the Camerouns (NCNC) which, though it had a tighter regional organization, still aimed at national leadership. British willingness to promote self-government aroused the more populous Northern region into defensive measures against a threat of dominance by the better-organized groupings in the Eastern and Western regions. The Northern Peoples' Congress (NPC) is a political party with some of the characteristics of the Democratic party in the southern states of the United States; that is, it serves primarily as an instrument for the protection of an endangered social structure. Leader of the NPC and premier of the Northern Region is the Sardauna of Sokoto, a descendant of the founder of the ruling Fulani aristocracy. Deputy leader Tafewa Balewa holds office as prime minister of the federation.

Once committed to party organization, however, the traditional leaders of the northern emirates discovered that the democratic process made inroads in their own domains. A group representing the new, educated, antifeudal element formed the Northern Elements Peoples' Union (NEPU) and entered into a temporary political alliance with Azikwe's NCNC. National politics has created strange bedfellows among these party groupings. In the 1959 elections, though the NPC won the largest number of seats (142), they failed to obtain a clear parliamentary majority. The NCNC-NEPU alliance came next with 82 seats and in the interest of national unity or political power formed a coalition government with their conservative rivals. This pattern, though unlikely to last, illustrates the advances that have been made from the deep tribal and social cleavages that separated these party groupings a few years ago. Apparently the progressive NEPU grouping in the north have been sacrificed at least temporarily to the power hunger of their eastern allies. However, true party politics on a national basis may result from these shiftings of loyalties within an independent Nigeria, shifts that from now on may prove too rapid and complex for outsiders to predict.

Chief Awolowo's Action Party, originally based on the Yoruba people of the Western Region, sought to become a national opposition party through adoption of extreme attitudes, dangerous to the new found unity of the nation. The Action party itself was split in the process and Awolowo and some of his followers were imprisoned for treason. Absence of a legitimate opposition, particularly in the Western region, provides grounds for further subversive movements. Each of the major party groupings are now in competition for the support of minor political formations, such as the Niger Delta Congress in the Eastern region, the United Emancipation League or the United Moslem party in Lagos Federal territory. In the opinion of a member of the new Nigerian intelligentsia, "it would appear that Nigerian political parties are now more national than before as a result of a process of regroupment that has just barely begun. This, indeed, may prove an important palliative for Nigerian disunity. It may offer a more organic sense of unity than that which is now provided by the formal framework of a federal constitution." [11]

Political Issues. The overwhelming issue in modern Nigeria is the winning of a lasting form of national unity. Now that the fight for self-government has been won, the union of all groups into a single people with common ends is essential in order to profit from independence. The bulk of the people are engaged in peasant agriculture. Before they will consent to abandon the security of their traditional social values, tribal and at best provincial, they need to be shown that better living conditions can be achieved here and now. Nigerian leaders are making imaginative efforts to educate their peoples regarding the benefits western technology will bring if they prepare themselves through social union. To make good on their promises, responsible administrations must be assured of a steady flow of far-seeing capital investment into their land. In consequence, the future viability of Nigeria as an independent African nation may rest largely in the hands of British and American finance. A further issue, perhaps of greater importance to the leadership élite than to the bulk of the population, is the question of Pan-Africanism. Events elsewhere in West Africa challenge the leadership of Nigeria as the largest, richest, and perhaps most stable aggregation of West African peoples. A temptation exists to plunge into an exciting if somewhat unreal arena of international politics based on a hypothetical economic, political, and cultural unification of the hitherto separated peoples of West Africa. Commitment to outside influences, communist, Arabic, or neoimperialist might result from any such premature adventures. Whether or not Nigeria sets her own pace of political and economic evolution from the colonial connection to full independence or surrenders her newly won sovereignty to an all African dream will be settled in the not too distant future.

GHANA

The coming of freedom for the black peoples of Africa was heralded by the creation of the independent state of Ghana. At least this is what the enthusiastic followers of Dr. Kwame Nkrumah believe, and to some extent their belief has shaped events both inside Ghana and in neighboring territories. The mantle of a political John the Baptist has proved embarrassing at times to this small nation, unimportant both economically and strategically and far from confident in the strength of its own social union. Gallant efforts to symbolize pan-African unity while struggling to accommodate representative government to tribalism in their own domains have led to some contradictions and confusions.

The Constitution of Ghana. Any appraisal of current political affairs in Ghana should start from the understanding that the new republic has a firm constitutional tradition. Independence was achieved largely through a process of constitution building and adaptation. The present republican constitution approved in principle by a popular plebiscite in July 1960 is an adaptation of the 1957 constitution granted by the British to inaugurate freedom. That in turn was a lineal descendant of the 1951 constitution recommended by the Coussey Commission as a basic pattern for self-government. Constitutionalism may be considered an inheritance from the British connection, willingly embraced by both leadership and community. That the first constitution, drawing authority directly from the popular will, should seek to embody African characteristics (express the African personality) appears in a sound tradition of constitutional growth.

The government have declared that their constitution is not copied from that of any other country but has been designed to meet the particular needs of Ghana and to express the realities of Ghana's constitutional position.[12] Though this assertion contains an element of truth, Western institutions, practices, and principles have been blended in a unique manner to render distinctiveness to an African variation. Ultimate sovereign authority is placed in the hands of an electorate established on the basis of universal suffrage. Important amendments of the constitution must be submitted to a popular referendum. Exercise of the powers of government rests in the hands of a legislature and executive chosen by majority vote of the electorate at regular intervals. The president, elected at the same time as the legislature, would normally be leader of the majority party. His status as ceremonial head of state does not limit his activities as partisan government leader. In this respect his office is analogous to the role of the Tudor monarchy in England, except, of course, as regards hereditary succession. The British system of ministerial responsibility to parliament has been continued, placing executive and legislative branches in a condition of mutual dependence subject to the will of the electorate for settlement of any dispute between them.

A novel concept of "greater union" has been introduced in Article 2 of the constitution. "In the confident expectation of an early surrender of sovereignty to a union of African states and territories, the people now confer on Parliament the power to provide for the surrender of the whole or any part of the sovereignty of Ghana." President Nkrumah has employed this elastic power to further his Pan-African concepts on the international level without seriously impinging on the domestic cohesion of his nation. Thus a meeting at Conakry in December 1960 between the presidents of Ghana, Guinea, and Mali resulted in the issue of an equivocal communiqué. "(We) have decided with a view to harmonize and co-ordinating the policies of our three states—

   1. To establish a union of our three states.
   2. To promote a common economic and monetary policy." [13]

It remains unclear, and is likely to be so for some time, what each or all of the presidents understood by a "union" or the nature of a "common economic and monetary policy."

Of greater practical significance in the constitution is Article 5 (1). "Ghana is a sovereign unitary Republic." Nkrumah's struggle against federalist claims within his new state has been perhaps the toughest of his career. Endorsement of a strict unitary character for the republic by an overwhelming popular vote represented a lasting triumph. However, the constitution does recognize (Article 8) a division into regions of which there are now eight. A provision of the 1957 constitution establishing regional assemblies has been reversed, though this change appears compromised by two equivocal articles. "There shall be a House of Chiefs for each Region of Ghana" (Article 50). "A House of Chiefs shall consist of such Chiefs, and shall have such functions relating to customary law and other matters, as may be provided by law" (Article 51). Under-representation of the Ashanti peoples in the dominant Convention People's party (CPP) has split the country on the proper functions to be retained by the traditional chieftaincies. The constitution does not embody a radical victory for anti-traditionalism. On the contrary it contains a declaration that may not be changed or mended except through popular referendum "that Chieftaincy in Ghana should be guaranteed and preserved" (Article 14).

Certain fundamental principles limiting the power of government are set out in the presidential declaration to be made on the assumption of office. These appear to have the force of a bill of rights subject to alteration only through a popular referendum. Among the more striking clauses are some analogous to basic American liberties. For example, "that no person should suffer discrimination on grounds of sex, race, tribe, religion, or political belief. . . . That subject to such restrictions as may be necessary for preserving public order, morality or health, no person

should be deprived of freedom of religion or speech, of
the right to move and assemble without hindrance or of
the right of access to courts of law; and that no person
should be deprived of his property save in accordance
with law, and that no law should be made by which a
person is deprived of his property without adequate compensation other than a law imposing taxation or prescrib-
ing penalties for offences or giving restitution for civil
wrongs or protecting health or property." [14] The power to
repeal this article is reserved to the people.

By and large, the pattern of government in the Republic of Ghana rests on a firm constitutional base. Emergence of the present constitution from colonial rule has
resulted in the continuance of powers and practices that
may appear arbitrary to Western eyes even though carried
out by a popularly elected government. Attention has been
drawn to arbitrary deportations for political purposes of
those unable to claim Ghanaian citizenship, as well as the
use of preventive detention orders in certain areas. In
December 1960, for example, preventive detention orders were made against 118 persons in the Ashanti and
other regions. However, this does not represent any innovation in police matters peculiar to an independent
Ghana. British colonial rule practiced similar forms of
control in tribal areas and personal liberties have not yet
won superior recognition to the need for public order.
From the juridical point of view, at least, the people control both the forms and practices of government in the
republic. If Ghana remains a one-party state, this is because a majority of the electorate so desire. Obstacles to
an opposition party victory, involving overthrow of the
existing régime, may not be attributed to the juridical
pattern of the state.

Political Parties. The ruling Convention People's party is
sometimes regarded as the personal following of Kwame
Nkrumah, reflecting his personality and the exigencies of
his career. This view oversimplifies political evolution in

tropical Africa. Ghana's prime minister himself would be more likely to borrow Sir Winston Churchill's declaration: "It was the nation and the race . . . that had the lion's heart. I had the luck to be called upon to give the roar."

The genius of the Gold Coast peoples has been operating to create political unity for self-government for the better part of a century of British rule. In 1871, enlightened leaders of the Fanti confederacy, meeting at the Mankesim conference, drew up a constitution along modern lines to promote social betterment and economic development. Though the colonial officials of the day failed to implement this constitution, it served as rallying point for the emergence of the Aborigines' Rights Protection Society, which sought to unite divergent tribal and social interests as a check on Colonial Office rule. A rapid increase in the numbers of an educated African middle class in Accra and other areas led to the formation of the West African National Congress and eventually to a nationalist movement, the United Gold Coast Convention. This latter body, based on a radical youth movement, gave Nkrumah his opportunity. Summoned from American and British studies by the Accra leaders to fill the post of organizing secretary, he soon widened the base and policies of the movement and renounced the leadership of the scholarly Dr. Danquah to found his own Convention People's party. This party, however, has always been and still is conditoned by its historic origins. It neither created nor monopolized nationalist feelings. The road it has followed to independence—or freedom, in Ghana's vocabulary—branched off, perhaps to make a successful shortcut, from a highway on which all the major groups of the community were traveling more slowly and with far less discipline.

Modernization, social as well as economic, has been the keynote of the party's success. The growth in numbers of educated, detribalized citizens who need political organization and nationalist feelings to replace lost kinship ties and tribal loyalties, has provided a dedicated core of party

workers. Whether these "new people" are firmly in control
of social power or whether the pace of change may provoke grave reaction is not yet decided. In the past the fight
for freedom proved an inestimable boon to the party by
adding emotional unity to the cohesiveness of the already
highly disciplined organization. When nationhood became
assured, a new generalized slogan was called for. Nkrumah
committed the party to "modernization," which seemed
to meet the psychological and economic needs of his followers while remaining sufficiently vague not to fetter
practical administration. If modernization moves fast
enough along economic and educational lines, the whole
community should be able to reintegrate itself on a different level. However, if it drags, social transition may
dramatize itself into political warfare, upsetting the stability of governments and weakening the direction of public policies.

Overdramatization of party loyalty remains an apparent
danger, at least to Western eyes. In a message sent to his
"comrades of the freedom fighting squads" in January
1961, Dr. Nkrumah declared, "I wish to emphasize again
today that the Convention People's Party is supreme in all
things. The Convention People's Party is Ghana and Ghana
is the Convention People's Party. I charge you all to stand
firm behind the Party. We went forward from Positive
Action to tactical action, now we go still forward from tactical action to double action. Every Ghanaian male and
female must tighten his belt and move forward in the
great exercise of double action. Ghana needs the services
of every man and woman and every Ghanaian must double his efforts to help to bring success to the effort of the
Party and Government in the social, economic, industrial
and cultural reconstruction of Ghana." [15] Though this language appears reminiscent of totalitarian organization, it
is addressed to people accustomed to strong tribal and
communal loyalties. Opposition parties have fared badly
partly because of their own failure to accept the limitations of legal and parliamentary action. Violence lies close

to the surface in a society in transition between tribal and national loyalties. Solidarity has taken at least the temporary form of one-party loyalty.

Major Issues. The direction of economic development underlies most of the important social and political issues in Ghana. Nkrumah describes himself as a Marxist Christian,° but this seems more of an autobiographical note than a declaration of policy binding on his party or government. The British set a pattern for the independent cocoa farmer by the institution of a cocoa marketing board. This organization was intended to protect individual producers from disastrous fluctuations in the world price of cocoa. Briefly, the board bought all cocoa grown in the country at a fixed price roughly guaranteed over a period of years and resold it on the world market. During the years of the postwar boom, the price paid the farmer was substantially below world prices. The accrued surplus was intended to insure guaranteed prices over a number of years should the market collapse. Gradually, however, this tempting income has been used by the government to finance agricultural improvements beyond the reach of individual producers. Nkrumah had the political audacity to continue the scheme despite previous denunciations of it as imperialist exploitation. The powerful Agricultural Development Corporation, as it is now called, is moving toward an agrarian revolution striking at the roots of traditional social organization more effectively than through shifts in political power.

As in most African communities, land tenure lies at the heart of the social structure. Though Ghana is blessed with a substantial small-farmer agriculture built around the cultivation of the cocoa bean, the largest landholdings remain in the hands of the tribal chiefs. This means that customary tenure still prevails, barring the advance of an exchange economy. The Convention People's party is leaning toward

° In his book *Consciencism,* published in 1964, Nkrumah endeavors to adapt Marxist philosophy to the African political situation.

a form of Domesday Book survey that would clear titles on the basis of individual ownership. Another policy is the encouragement of coöperative farms in a manner not unlike Soviet experiments.

As Ghana is still primarily a peasant economy and is likely to remain one for many decades, the direction of her agrarian reforms is of considerable interest to Western sympathizers. If the pace is set too fast and requires forceful action against traditional opposition, the government may find itself approximating communist states in the methods to which it is driven. Links with Western standards and investments channels might be sacrificed. At this critical juncture the expert experience and technical skills of American agricultural specialists might prove invaluable in exploring alternative solutions.

SIX

•••••••••••••••••••••••••••••

INDEPENDENT STATES—

FRENCH-SPEAKING

Though independence for African peoples has mounted as a continent-wide wave, solidarity for freedom has not encompassed similarity of institutional expression. Countries formerly under British tutelage have continued to a considerable degree an organic adaptation of long-standing governmental processes to a specific African environment. However, the great areas of West Africa, conditioned by the Latin culture of France and Belgium, lacked in some measure this evolutionary tradition. Their colonial directors served as architects or sculptors of social institutions; constitutional edifices were presented wholly constructed, graced in some instances with European refinements, but lacking solid foundations in any bedrock of indigenous political experience. Consequently the immediate future of political structures in French-speaking[1] areas of tropical Africa lies within a field of cautious speculation. Evidences of continuity and future direction exist in terms of previous political evolution during the colonial period, in light of basic economic and social necessities of the region as a whole, and perhaps more obscurely through the rapidly changing character of the social and political élites replacing the once-dominant European image. The present effervescence of political personalities, parties, and policies provides a dramatic, though not very comprehensible, accompaniment to the settlement of unresolved situations. Perhaps of greatest import to a Western observer is the question of the final mold into which governmental patterns may be resolved. Elements of authoritarian, one-party dominance verging on totalitarianism manifest themselves alongside representative forms rooted in loose ethnic and village confederations of interest. Political instrumentalities inherited from the past and adapted to African circumstances may prove a decisive factor in determining final constitutional choice. The degree to which they are retained and utilized at the moment provides one useful clue to future developments. In all probability the future of African nationalism as a world force will depend on the size of the regional groupings capable of achieving the unity of nationhood. Issues of federation, confederation, or "Balkanization" lie in the foreground of African politics. Less predictable are movements to seize and stabilize power centers for social, economic, and ethnic groupings. The fluidity of the current élites introduces a kaleidoscopic character to any survey of party politics in action throughout former French or Belgian possessions in tropical Africa.

THE SHAPING OF FRENCH-SPEAKING AFRICA

France alone of European nations in Africa was vouchsafed a clear vision of a *mission civilisatrice* (civilizing mission). Contact between French and African communities has been marked by an intent to establish a permanent relationship, an intent that even now remains under serious consideration by African peoples. No other Western nation has made comparable efforts to share its cultural heritage with the emerging civilizations of tropical Africa. An outlook, however, does not constitute accomplishment or guarantee successful fulfillment. It remains questionable whether metropolitan France possesses sufficient economic power or enough devoted men to serve as an exclusive source of development for former African territories. The indigenous inhabitants, in their urgent need to catch up with the rest of the world, cannot afford the luxury of sentiment.

Constitutional Forms. While the concept of an interfusion of cultures may be held central to the history of French overseas expansion, the specific form it has taken in Africa today may be dated from the Brazzaville Conference of 1944. The significance of this African conference, called by General de Gaulle before the liberation of metropolitan France, is only now becoming apparent. It was at her cultural peripheries that France found the strength for self-restoration. The Chad province of Equatorial Africa, under its African governor, Felix Éboue, proclaimed itself for De Gaulle in 1940, while the metropolitan French were submitting to Pétain. Brazzaville signified the first of the succession of compromises that, starting with recognition of the dignity and rights of African peoples through provision for political consultation on the level of local assemblies, ended with acceptance of total political independence. A token admission of African representatives to the national legislature of France began an integration of French and African political parties that exercised definite influence on the future character of African states and statesmen.

The Loi Cadre *of 1956.* The unfinished business of the Brazzaville Conference was given a great step forward in 1956 when a basic political reform was enacted under the name of the *Loi Cadre* or *Loi Deferre*. This law took the form of an enabling act to be filled in later by decree. In 1957 a series of decrees established a French version of self-government for tropical African territories. The general pattern adopted involved the creation of a *Conseil du Gouvernement* (council of government) in each territory to assume policy-making powers along executive lines. The councils were composed of four members elected by the territorial assembly and three nominated by the Governor, who acted as president of the council. Council members were given ministerial rank. The territorial assemblies, whose powers had been largely deliberative and consultative up to that time, had their fields widened to cover all territorial matters, except those expressly reserved by law for the central government. It would be a mistake to regard these changes as establishing legislative supremacy on the part of autonomous colonial legislatures. The decision-making element in French overseas government remained, as before, in the executive organs of administration. Councils of government replaced, to a considerable extent, the authority of a governor, who had come to act increasingly as the agent of a métropolitan bureaucracy. For all practical purposes, the council of government, once established, was independent of the territorial assembly. The latter, more of an advisory body than a law-making institution, had effective investigatory and supervisory powers to examine details of administrative policy and behavior. It should be noted as significant to future development and parliamentary forms in free African states that functions of the territory assemblies did not encompass formulation of general rules of policy—that remained in the province of the administrative decree.

From the French Union to the French Community. By a gesture unique in the relationship between European and African peoples since the times of Imperial Rome, the 1946 constitution of the Fourth Republic, in creating *l'Union Française,* granted full French citizenship to all African subjects of France. This involved at least the educated African minority in the domestic politics and party organization of metropolitan France. Though the degree of representation granted overseas citizenry was largely illusory in terms of influencing policies in Paris, its educational and cultural results may possess profound influence on future relations between free Africa and her former metropole.

The 1958 constitution of the Fifth Republic provided that the African communities be given a choice between true autonomy within a newly created *Communauté* (Community) and outright independence. Though only Guinea opted for complete separation, the vague community tie weighed lightly on the realities of African freedom after 1958. Article One of the constitution of the Fifth Republic declared that "the Community shall be based on the equality and solidarity of the peoples composing it." This obviously impractical assumption prohibited setting in motion any workable community organization on a hierarchical basis. In 1960 a realistic amendment to the 1958 constitution provided for the sovereign independence of community members. All the African states of French origin opted for this status which admitted them to full membership of the United Nations. Bonds between the French and African peoples, now largely uncluttered by legal obligations on either side, remained rooted on a firm basis of cultural affinity and economic advantage. This severance of constitutional ties does not appear to have affected the measure of support continued by France in the way of economic privileges and financial and technical aid.

West Africa of French Expression. Former French West Africa (AOF: *Afrique Occidentale Française*) was never a combination of peoples resulting from the initiative of the indigenous inhabitants. Its creation may be credited to a distinguished line of French administrators. Its population, roughly estimated at 25,000,000, is contained in an area of nearly 2,000,000 square miles, comprising Mauretania, Senegal, Guinea, Mali, Ivory Coast, Upper Volta, Niger, and Dahomey. Though the federation conceived for the convenience of colonial administration has collapsed, necessities of coöperation underlie a continuous maneuvering of politicians, parties, and ethnic groups toward forms of closer union. At present two tentative groupings are engaged in experimental assays as to the future development of regional unity along political lines. Fired by the somewhat racist doctrine of Pan-Africanism, Guinea and Mali

seek to cross linguistic and geographic lines in an association with Ghana for the purpose of pioneering the widest
possible union of free African peoples. This may be char-
acterized as a strictly political approach based on the
charismatic fervor of a leadership élite and loosely related
to specific, practical needs of the territories in question.
The more legitimate successors to the old federation—
Ivory Coast, Niger, Dahomey, and the Upper Volta—
have formed a loose confederation of states under the title
of the *Conseil de l'Entente.* A Customs Union and Solidarity Fund are the principal achievements of this association. In April 1961, the members of the *Entente* signed a
treaty of coöperation with France. Though the terms of
this treaty were concerned for the most part with economic and financial matters, military agreements permitting the stationing of French forces on African soil were
included by all the signatories except Upper Volta. On
political questions touching on military or international
alignments, the *Conseil de l'Entente* appears to be losing
its importance to wider groupings extending beyond the
limits of the former AOF. The Brazzaville bloc of 12
French-speaking African states was formed in October
1960. Senegal, divorced from the short-lived Mali Federation, was enabled to express her interest in African unity
in conjunction with Mauretania, the Ivory Coast, Upper
Volta, Niger, Dahomey, Chad, Gabon, the Central African
Republic, the Congo Republic (Brazzaville), and the Indian Ocean island, the Malagasy Republic. Accomplishments of the Brazzaville group, which has now named itself Union of African States and Madagascar, include pro-
nouncements on African relations to France, the Congo
(Leopoldville), and other international concerns. Perhaps
more significant are plans for an Inter-State Economic
Secretariat, mutual defense pacts, and joint action in the
promotion of investments and relations with the European
Economic Community. The advancement of Pan-Africanism through ambitious projects of political unification appears of slight interest to the Brazzaville group. The Casa-

blanca grouping, in which Guinea, Mali, and Ghana represent tropical·Africa, are more concerned with far-reaching plans for the advancement of Pan-Africanism involving Morocco, Algeria, the United Arab Republic, and a reunified Congo Republic (Leopoldville). This association lacks much of the infra structure of common economic interest and practical propinquity that serves to give cohesion to the Brazzaville bloc. The former United Nations Trust territory, French Togo, remains uncommitted outside these two groupings.

As an immediate political issue, the question of federation for the former French West African territories is losing much of its meaning. Divisions between African states based on previous colonial connections or even language distinctions are breaking down. The emergence into independence of mighty entities, such as Nigeria with its 35,000,000 inhabitants, is changing the balance of political and economic power throughout the whole region. Perhaps of greatest significance is the appearance of a distinctively African conception of national sovereignty which avoids much of the rigid exclusiveness of the Western tradition. Among Africans, mutual interdependence, cooperation, and even identification may take place beyond the bounds of state nationalism. Sovereign states constitute to the African mere instruments for the attainment of wider freedoms long denied in the economic, social, and cultural fields. Until such time as attachment to a particular state overshadows a prevailing sense of being African, liable to exploitation by other peoples and in urgent need of technological advancement, questions of state sovereignty may be subordinated on pragmatic grounds to the pursuit of wider, more realistic objectives.

Constitutional Configurations. Among the *Entente* states constitutional similarities outweigh divergencies. Prevailing presidential systems echo to some extent the decree-making power of previous colonial governors. A certain logic of institutional continuity appears to have exercised more influence than abstract theories of democracy on the forms of government adopted. Thus the initiative in formulating laws and policies remains with the executive in the person of the president; legislatures are largely advisory and supervisory bodies in the tradition of the former territorial assemblies. Representative forms of government follow the experience of the people in their tribal and party groupings rather than blueprints based on the doctrines of Rousseau or John Stuart Mill. Thus, in both the Ivory Coast and Dahomey, elections are held not for individual candidates but to choose a chief of state, the president, and a party to support him. Votes are cast for a party slate headed by the presidential candidate. The slate receiving a majority vote from the electorate captures all seats in a unicameral legislature. Though this electoral system precludes responsible party government as practiced in Western lands, it is not necessarily antagonistic to representative principles. As long as elections remain free, the majority group in the community is represented without hindrance in the seats of power. Use of the referendum on a thoroughly popular basis is a concomitant part of ideas of representation in these new lands. In Upper Volta and Niger, for example, a popular referendum bestowed on the national legislatures the right to select the first presidents of the republics for full five-year terms.

The Republic of Senegal after three years experience with a balanced political system based on division of power between executive and legislative organs and contending political parties has revised its Constitution to provide for a Presidential system of government and virtual single party control. This retreat from precepts of Western democracy by one of the more politically experienced African communities reflects some of the difficulties encountered in attempting to establish advanced political techniques upon an inadequate economic base. The particular occasion was an attempt by the Premier, Mamadou Dia to overthrow the National Assembly in the interests of his program of rapid economic reform. President Senghor,

one of the wisest and most experienced of African statesmen, rallied the security forces against the projected coup
d'etat and won support at a popular referendum for a
more authoritarian constitution. The realities of African
politics remain so close to economic and social tensions
that the maintenance of order and national unity generally necessitates the sacrifice of party rivalries. The authority of the group and its leader in African tradition remains absolute until repudiated by an effective majority.
Provisions for universal suffrage, a wide use of the referendum, and lack of oppressive police power generally en-
sures final authority for the determination of governmental forms and policies remaining in the hands of a popular
majority. Representative government under African circumstances means representation of African society in
terms of its operative forms and attitudes, conditioned by
decades of colonial domination, and rooted in tribal cohesion and respect for leadership of its own choice.

Equatorial Africa. With the exception of prosperous Gabon
(a prosperity based on timber, oil, and minerals), former
French Equatorial Africa may be accounted impoverished
even in terms of a not conspicuously hopeful West African
economy. Chad, the Central African Republic, and the
Republic of the Congo (Brazzaville) face economic and
social problems that are unlikely to find solution in terms
of their separate existences as sovereign entities. In practice they have achieved a considerable degree of economic
integration and coöperation, though resulting benefits are
curtailed through the unwillingness of Gabon to pool her
resources with those of her more destitute neighbors.
L'Union des Républiques d'Afrique Centrale, which the
three states sought to maintain alone after the secession
of Gabon, has been largely abandoned in favor of the
Brazzaville bloc of which Gabon is a member.

Constitutional arrangements dating from 1960 in all
these states are remarkably similar. A conservative cling-
ing to French inherited ideals and political structures ap-

pears a distinguishing feature of Equatorial Africa. Thus all four Republics describe themselves in their constitutions as "indivisible, democratic and social." Official national mottoes are indicative of continuing bias toward a French outlook. The Central African Republic has chosen "Unity, Dignity, Work"; Gabon, "Unity, Work, Justice"; and the Brazzaville Congo, "Unity, Work, Progress." The principle of popular sovereignty, enforced through universal suffrage and referendums, is generally recognized. Strong executive control of the government along the lines of the French Fifth Republic is the accepted pattern. In Gabon, Chad, and the Congo (Brazzaville), the president is also prime minister. As in French-speaking West Africa, actualities of political control are vested in the single-party system that remains open to replacement by majority vote.

Togo and the Camerouns. Because of their former status as United Nations Trust territories, the French-speaking areas of Togo and the Camerouns have remained outside the groupings of former French colonial lands. However, from the institutional point of view they share a like framework of political concepts and administrative devices. Togo may be distinguished from its neighbors by an unusual degree of social and political solidarity stemming perhaps from the achievements of a particularly able prime minister, Sylvanus Olympio. It remains nevertheless a single-party state in which opposition is likely to receive scant toleration until it is in position to overthrow the ruling party by majority vote.[*]

The French Camerouns have had the most chequered political history of all former French possessions in tropical Africa. During the last years of trusteeship control, armed risings were carried out by radical tribal groupings

[*] The assassination of Olympio in 1963 by disgruntled veterans brought into power a regime that failed to win recognition by several of Togo's powerful neighbors as a legitimate government. Subsequently, however, the military junta achieved constitutional status through a popular referendum and reaffirmed Togo's close economic and political ties with France.

linked with anti-French forces in the United Arab Republic and North Africa. These rebellions continued after independence in the form of a civil war. The death, in November 1960, of Felix Moumie, the instigator of the rebellion, has been followed by effective pacification of most of the areas. The present government, headed by President Ahmadou Ahidjo, is based primarily on northern tribal groupings. It has succeeded in linking Cameroun with the Brazzaville bloc both for economic coöperation and support of the régime. The February 1961 plebiscite in the British Trust territory of the Cameroons resulted in the southern division opting for the Cameroun Republic, while the northern sector joined itself to Nigeria. Though the former French and British possessions retain distinctions, reflected in institutional organization, the Federal Republic of Cameroun may be accounted the first successful bi-lingual state to be established among the independent nations of southern Africa.

The Malagasy Republic. The Indian ocean island of Madagascar, 241,094 square miles in area, supports a population of approximately 5,000,000 people of diverse ethnic origin who have entered the island in successive waves from Malaysia. A common Indonesian language and similar religious practices provide closer social bonds than might be found among tribal groups on the mainland. Sixty years of French rule has created institutional and cultural ties with other elements in French-speaking Africa. However, Malagasy, both as regards its social solidarity and cultural differentiation, is in a different category from that of other nations sprung from France's tropical African empire. Though associated with the Brazzaville group, it is probable that Malagasy considers her ties to France unique and not subject to bloc politics. In her internal constitutional arrangements, Malagasy betrays less pressure toward centralized concentration of political power than is the case with other new African nations doubtful of the strength of their social union. The president of the republic is indirectly elected by an electoral college composed of members of parliament and delegates from the Provincial Councils and municipal and rural assemblies. Parliament is bicameral with a senate representative of provincial and local territorial units. The island is divided into six provinces, each of which boasts an elected General Council. An appointee of the central government, a secretary of state delegate, serves as executive officer for each Provincial Council. The founder president, Philibert Tsiranana, and his dominant *Parti Social Démocrate Malgache* have as their only serious rival a Communist-front organization using an indigenous nomenclature with the initials AKFM.

Mauretania. The Islamic Republic of Mauretania, approximately the size of Washington, Oregon, California, and Nevada combined (and a great deal more desolate), has a population of 650,000, of which approximately 500,000 are nomadic Moors of Arab-Berber origin. With virtually no political experience of its own—its administrative capital was in Senegal until 1957—neglected economic development, and an acute shortage of educated, indigenous administrators, the only visible capital the new republic may be said to have lies in the courage of its young men among whom may be numbered its President Mokhtar Ould Daddah. Mauretania may prove a testing ground for the influence of newly independent tropical Africa against the pull of traditional North Africa. At present Mauretania is in the Brazzaville group and tied closely to France for economic aid. However, Morocco denies the legitimacy of her territorial independence and Islamic nationalists throughout North Africa may struggle to partition her area by soliciting the loyalty of her nomads. From the political point of view, Mauretania is likely to serve for several decades as an uneasy frontier between Black Africa and the Mediterranean North.

Economic Bases of Politics. In general the French-speaking states of Africa are geographically artificial, underpopulated, industrially undeveloped, and unable to provide essential skills and acceptable standards of living from their own separate resources. Economic solidarity through customs unions, common transportation systems, and coördinated investment planning appears a *sine qua non* of technological growth. Without such growth the rising expectations of the freed peoples cannot be satisfied and present political structures would be shattered. Political leaders are well aware of these realities underlying their grip on power; much of the present maneuvering is concerned with which group will obtain the initiative in an inevitable movement toward economic integration. Another factor, partially concealed behind assertions of independence mixed with denunciations of the colonial era, is a continuing dependence on France for day-to-day economic stability. Metropolitan France took to heart the lesson of Guinea and has avoided disruption of the flow of direct aid and pre-independence trade concessions to her other erstwhile dependents. Former subsidies are largely continued after independence under the nomenclature of *Fonds d'Investissement et Developpement Economique et Sociale* (FIDES). The direction of trade remains firmly tied to France and to a lesser extent her partners in the European Economic Community (the Common Market). The Common Market has also created a development fund for associated territories (FEDOM) to which new African nations may look for needed investments. In general, French-speaking Africans are not obsessed by suspicions of French economic neocolonialism. Generous treatment of Mali, even when it was flirting economically with the Soviet bloc, has allayed fears of political pressure tied to economic aid. Besides, where else could the new nations look if they interrupted well-established trade patterns with France? Realities of this bread-and-butter nature tend to further harmonious institutional continuities with the former metropolitan power, operating smoothly below the level of political declamations made for home consumption, and to echo on the sounding board of the United Nations.

Party Politics. Party systems in French-speaking Africa may be described conservatively as a specialized study.[2] A major consideration lies in the interterritorial character of party organization carried over from the days of African solidarity in the struggle for independence. The history of the *Rassemblement Démocratique Africain* (RDA), which at one time had branches in all French West African countries except Mauretania, is essential to an understanding of the evolution of many of the present national parties. Another element is the influence of French political parties, particularly those of the Left, during the period they were linked to African affiliates. Perhaps the most important ingredient of all is the skillful blending of ethnic and linguistic interests carried out by indigenous politicians to provide themselves with a secure base of power. Economic and social viewpoints appear to be subordinated to personalities and regional groupings in party structures.

Three major contributions of party organization to the political system of French-speaking Africa may be postulated. In the first place their interterritorial origins have made them instruments of African solidarity above and beyond limitations of nationhood. Second, they have proved effective means of linking ethnic and regional interest groups together in terms of wider social and national purposes. Third, they have provided the mechanism by which an educated minority could establish themselves as a political élite. The volatile nature of the present party structure (apart from its French cast of mind) is due in part to the changing nature of this élite. A generation of African Frenchmen, symbolized perhaps by Houphouët-Boigny and Leopold Senghor, is being challenged by restless, ambitious youth influenced more strictly by local African sentiment and personal career considerations. It is impracticable to foretell the future form of the political party structure in French-speaking Africa except to guess that it will be a much more closely disciplined system than is usual in Western countries. Discipline will be essential because for many years ahead it will be needed as a binding force to hold loosely joined tribal elements into the pattern of a modern state. Moral authoritarianism may prove the only practical replacement for the traditional authoritarianism of tribal chief and colonial ruler.

THE CONGO REPUBLIC (LEOPOLDVILLE)

Events in the Congo are comprehensible only in terms of the institutional history of the region. The cruel intrusion of King Leopold's filibustering company in the 1880's wrought further havoc in an already chaotic social economy devastated by the slave trade. Within the 905,000 square miles annexed for private exploitation dwelt 70 major ethnic groups subdivided into hundreds of clans speaking approximately 400 dialects. When the Belgian government assumed responsible control in 1908, it faced a grim task in cleaning up the pitiful shambles left by the unrestricted "free enterprise" of the nineteenth century. Humanitarian business management, or, in the words of Belgium's greatest colonial administrator, Governor General Ryckmans, *Dominer pour Servir* (Rule in Order to Serve), became the rigid framework for Belgian control. In practice this meant bureaucratic supremacy responsible only to the ministries and legislature in Brussels. Underlying the dogma of impartial and efficient administration for the welfare of the indigenous inhabitants and the balancing of the colonial budget lay the realities of great economic concessions. Among these privileged monopolies major rank may be given to the *Union Minière du Haut Katanga,* controlling the copper mines of Katanga, *Forminière* with its virtual diamond monopoly, and *Huilever* linked to the British company Unilever in the exploitation of tropical vegetable oils. The financial structure underpin-

ning this great complex for tropical exploitation, though
centered in Brussels, may be considered international in
terms of its ultimate ownership with British and American
shareholders playing an important if undetermined part. A
certain degree of autonomy was accorded this Big Business
interest in its handling of Congolese resources. Certainly
administrators were influenced and limited in their policy
determinations by an intermingling of financial and political power in the metropolitan capital. It is significant that
the powerful Socialist party, even when holding office,
never developed any plan in accordance with its own
avowed principles, for the democratization of the Congo
régime. Achievements in the development of natural resources and even in raising indigenous standards of living
were considerable. Arguments as to the degree to which
Belgian interests, private and public, profited at the expense of human progress in the Congo are likely to remain
unsettled for many years. It is perhaps worth pointing out
that a vast infra structure of roads, railways, ports, power
plants, manufacturing facilities, and educational and health
services must be laid down as a capital investment in primitive communities before dividends in the form of social
improvements can be returned to the inhabitants. In comparison with former French and British possessions in
West or Central Africa, the Belgians could claim a satisfactory and often superior record of economic advancement. For example the primary school system encompassed
half the child population of the 13,500,000 Africans, a
figure almost double that in comparable French territories.
The index of indigenous consumption rose from 100 in
1950 to 176 in 1857.[3] Matters touching the social dignity
of the inhabitants, however, were indifferently handled.
Condescending paternalism on the part of the administering bureaucracy resulted in practical segregation and de-
nial of social participation to the African majority. As
regards the ordinary Belgian *colon*, particularly the lower-
class Flemish artisan, his attitude seldom rose above the
"bootblack" concept common to white settlers throughout

tropical Africa. A notable and powerful exception may be made in favor of the Roman Catholic Church to which was entrusted a virtual monopoly of primary education. Twenty percent of the active European residents in the Congo were members of the clergy.

Describing an area almost the size of Europe as a gigantic "company town," though perhaps straining an analogy beyond legitimate bounds, has its uses in understanding some of the consequences of the Belgian system of rule. Lack of opportunity to participate in the social as well as political organization of community life paralyzed the initiative of the indigenous inhabitants. The always-difficult transition from subsistence agriculture under tribal or clan conditions into modern technological society involves a great ferment of social activity. Higher education and party politics provide two of the most practical training grounds for the leaders and directors of the new society. Both channels were denied to the Congolese under a system oriented to regard people in terms of a "labor force." In this respect the Belgian régime denigrated its role to that of a caretaker for international finance.

From the institutional point of view the division of the country into six provinces made for sound administration, while considerable latitude for autonomy on the part of provincial governments was countered by the unity and hierarchical discipline prevailing within the controlling bureaucracy. Integration of these provinces and their ethnic components into a unified state, however, required the cohesion of indigenous groupings along national lines in terms of political parties or social movements. Failure of the Belgian administration to realize this necessity inhibited the emergence of a Congolese nation from the cocoon of a colonial, administrative entity. Apart from administrative organization, government in the Belgian Congo rested on the force supplied by the *Force Publique,* recruited among generally illiterate Africans and officered wholly by Belgians. Here again an unfortunate analogy may be drawn with the institution of a "company police." Starting out in

barbarous fashion as the mercenary bullies of Leopold's
infamous company, the *Force Publique* never achieved
more than a surface discipline. Unlike the French army
there was no evangelical fervor of a civilizing mission to
link its officer corps to a social purpose held in common
for and with their African soldiery. The British practice of
drawing police power from the local organization of the
inhabitants was equally foreign to a highly centralized
bureaucracy that preferred to rely on mobile forces separated from the daily life of the inhabitants. Collapse of
the institutional network of government created by the
Belgians may be laid directly to this failure in the structure
of police power.

The Nationalist Movement. Congolese nationalism was not
fertilized in its early stages by fruitful contact with European liberalism to the extent that occurred in British and
French territories. In fact, the policy of the Belgian bureaucracy was to sequester their wards within an ideological *cordon sanitaire*, uncorrupted by travel abroad or contact with disturbing European radicalism. In consequence,
the *évolués*, products of a parsimonious system of local
secondary education, gravitated into practical and con-
spiratorial politics without becoming exposed to political
philosophies. As one-quarter of the population of the
Congo had become urbanized by the 1950's in the semi-
industrialized towns of Leopoldville, Stanleyville, Elisa-
bethville, and Jadotville, party organization could be
linked to immediate problems of jobs, wages, and living
conditions for African workers. For example, the formation
of Joseph Kasavubu's Abako party in 1956 coincided with
a rise in unemployment and cuts in already inadequate
wage levels. This grouping, whose formal title is the "Association of the Bakongo," provides a clue to the nature of
subsequent Congolese politics. Belgian administration had
developed segregated indigenous quarters round the European centers of the cities. These quarters were encouraged to retain tribal associations and through later devel-

opment of elective and partially autonomous borough councils became tribal power centers. Thus Kasavubu's people, the Bakongo, who numbered 800,000 in the Lower Congo, considered that they should exercise predominant power in Leopoldville. On this basis of tribal self-interest and solidarity, a nucleus of party opposition to the colonial régime could be raised in a manner that attracted support from other tribal groupings and looser associations. Residents of any large American city are familiar with the process of language and ethnic group alliances in municipal politics. Lacking an umbrella of sophisticated national movements, Congolese politicians had to advance their municipal aggregations onto a national level. Patrice Lumumba made a bold effort from the start of his *Mouvement National Congolais* (MNC) to create a nontribal nationalist movement along lines similar to those used by Ghana's Congress party. Perhaps events moved too fast; in 1959 the metropolitan government conceded local and provincial elections causing a rash of parties to spring up overnight. As the majority of these parties were based on tribes, aggregations of tribes, or special economic interest groups, the solidarity of a single national party became almost impossible to attain.

Independence. The rapid sequence of events that led through the riots of 1959 to the Brussels Round Table Conference of January 1960 and subsequent independence elections of June 1960 are matters of current history. Their interpretation in terms of the dramatic sequel provided by the United Nations intervention must await settlement of contemporary divisions of opinion.[4]

However, an institutional structure in the form of a provisional constitution for the new country was transferred in the process of the divestiture of Belgian sovereignty. This constitution possessed many weaknesses; as a transitional document it was promulgated under the authority of the departing Belgians to serve as the framework for the functioning of an indigenous constitutional convention.

Further the major clauses determining basic structure of the independent state were left so deliberately vague that no certain guide was provided to the degree of centralization, federal or unitary, considered essential to national solidarity. Nevertheless, the resolutions of the Brussels Round Table Conference formed the basis on which rested claims to the future legitimacy of succeeding regimes. As all the leading proponents of Congolese parties were present and voting at the conference, the ensuing document must have embodied at least a compromise of their views.

Principal features of the 1960 constitution were, first, the designation of the two houses of the Congolese Parliament as a Constituent Assembly. Constitutional legitimacy must accordingly stem from action on the part of this body. In the second place the Republic of the Congo was constituted as a unitary state composed of six provinces with provisions for provincial assemblies and a division of powers between central and provincial governments. Though the powers of the central government were enumerated, inadequate provisions were made for the inevitable conflicts between central and provincial authority. National institutions included a president, acting as chief of state and commander-in-chief of the armed forces with power to appoint and dismiss the ministry, subject to the approval of parliament. Possession of this power became a matter of vital importance in the struggle between President Kasavubu and Prime Minister Lumumba as United Nations forces considered themselves bound to recognize the constitutional validity of Kasavubu's actions. The government, headed by a prime minister, was intended to be responsible to parliament on policy matters. Parliament consisted of a House of Representatives, elected by universal suffrage on the basis of one representative for every 100,000 inhabitants, together with a senate composed of members designated by the provincial legislature on the basis of 14 per province. This parliament, in which no party held a majority, functioned to select Patrice Lumumba as prime minister and Joseph Kasavubu as president. Thereafter it disintegrated in the general chaos resulting from the mutiny of the *Force Publique* and the secession of Katanga province. All the complicated constitutional provisions ensuring the protection of Belgian property and the civil rights of Belgian residents sank without trace in the ten days succeeding July 8, 1960.

The Issue of Federalism. It remains obvious that, whether under a national or international régime, the Congo can never become a viable state until the question of federation, confederation, or separation of its constituent elements is settled. During the Belgian régime the Congo territory was an administrative and economic unit and little else. No tradition of unity based on participation of local communities in national affairs was cultivated by the colonial administration. Accordingly, the "national idea" needed to cement the peoples of the new state into a homogeneous political entity was constituted for the most part from a blend of anti-Europeanism, desire for freedom, and vague Pan-Africanism. It was the latter element that inspired Lumumba and his supporters both within and outside the Congo to press for a centralized state overriding regional, ethnic, and cultural divisions. On the other hand, Tshombe of Katanga and Albert Kalonji of Kasai represented a separatist outlook based on a widespread reluctance of tribal and conservative groups to submit to forced unification. The challenge of Gizenga, Lumumba's self-proclaimed heir, and his Stanleyville régime to the legitimacy of the national government sponsored by Kasavubu at Leopoldville complicated the issue. Soviet, Arab, and some African backing of Gizenga's pretensions raised the question onto an international level. When this turmoil, in part caused by the intrusion of Cold War maneuvering into the Congo situation, has subsided, it is likely that the reality of a choice between federation and confederation will become apparent. Federalism appears to be gaining and the issue may soon narrow down to whether a loose federal system providing for considerable provincial autonomy will prevail over concepts of nationalistic federalism tending toward centralized control.

Another vital question that may endanger the structure of the new state centers around the components of a federal system. The six original provinces contain aggregations of ethnic groups that in many instances would like to set up political boundaries of their own. A resurgence of tribal-based politics might dismember the Congo into an unworkable association of jealous clans. Maneuverings of Congolese political and military chieftains since the death of Lumumba rival the politics of Italian city states during the Renaissance. When the personal safety of members of the warring factions can be sufficiently guaranteed by United Nations forces or otherwise, parliament may be expected to reassemble and reach some decision on the basic constitutional problem of federation. Thereafter truly national parties will become a necessity if the new state is to survive within its present boundaries.

United Nations Intervention. A new chapter in African politics was opened by the presence of a United Nations force in the Congo in July 1960. Invited originally by Prime Minister Lumumba to counter Belgian paratroopers reëntering to protect harassed Belgian residents, the United Nations Command eventually had to serve as an impartial arbiter between warring factions. Events are too recent to attempt any evaluation of this mission except along the most general lines. In the first place a negative task was performed of blocking separate intervention by either Soviet, Western, or African powers. This may be regarded as a landmark in African history to some extent reversing the European partition of the sub-continent inaugurated at the Berlin Conference of 1884. Second, it was demonstrated that basic administrative and economic order could be preserved by international technicians in the absence both of former colonial personnel and trained indigenous replacements. One of the traditional arguments against granting immediate independence to African peoples was thereby refuted. The administrative experience of United Nations officialdom gained in the Congo operation may prove of inestimable value when similar crises arise, as they threaten to do, in the Portuguese provinces of Angola and Mozambique.

Politically United Nations intervention settled nothing but simply averted disaster until such times as indigenous political rivals could simmer down and agree to work together for the survival of their country. Internal strains within the United Nations itself, the repudiation of the secretariat by the Soviet bloc, unilateral policies on the part of Belgium, the United Arab Republic, Guinea, and Ghana, paralyzed firm action in favor of any one faction. On the whole this may have proved fortunate, as the commitment of United Nations forces to any specific governmental structure in the Congo might have smacked of international imperialism. Perhaps the most effective side of United Nations intervention was its almost miraculous preservation of the dissolving economy of the country. In June 1961, when announcing a $10,000,000 United Nations loan to the Kasavubu régime to purchase needed imports, Secretary General Hammarskjöld was able to comment that "the grievous stage" had passed in the Congo. The later catastrophe leading to Hammarskjöld's death added a tragic postscript to this statement.

Future of Congolese Politics. Indications concerning the future political and social order in the Congo may be summarized in terms of likely continuities. In the first place the basic integrity of the territory will probably be preserved under a moderate or weak federal structure. United Nations action appears to have scotched external designs to carve up the young nation into tribal regions under foreign influence. Internally both the logic of economics and of developing national sentiment exert increasing pressure in favor of political unification. Second, national political parties, perhaps with regional bases along Nigerian lines, seem certain to emerge from the mutual destruction of

warring cliques. Third, effective administration will gain
in importance over political maneuvers once the educational efforts of the United Nations training echelons be-
gin to show results. In general, because of its size, diver-
sity, and rich economic resources, the Congo appears more
likely to conform to the flexible pattern of Nigeria than to
the rigid nationalism of Ghana or the jealous interplay of
other French-speaking states. An uncertain note may be
introduced by speculation on the future of the bordering
territory of Portuguese Angola. If, as seems probable, this
area erupts in a manner necessitating direct United Nations intervention, the whole concept of proper divisions of
African nationalist organization throughout the region may
be altered. The Congo may choose to become part of a
wider African aggregation of peoples. To the ordinary
inhabitant for whom Congolese nationalism is principally
a concomitant of African freedom, this would not entail
revolutionary change.

Rwanda-Burundi. Until 1960 the trust territory of Rwanda-
Burundi was linked in administrative and customs union
with the Belgian Congo. Efforts on the part of the Belgian
administration during 1959 to prepare the separate inhabitants of Rwanda and Burundi for some form of local autonomy stimulated tribal upheavals. The numerically superior Bahutu peoples of Rwanda rose against their overlord
tribe, the Batutsi, and expelled the official ruler, Mwami
Kigere V. The General Assembly of the United Nations
disagreed with the Belgian Trust administration's acceptance of this state of affairs and recommended the return
of the Mwami pending a referendum to settle the form of
government. In the meantime, however, in both Rwanda
and Burundi, provisional governments had been set up. In
Rwanda the Parmehut party supported by the Bahutu
tribe organized an electoral college out of communal coun-
cilors, elected a legislature and government, and pro-
ceeded to adopt a constitution proclaiming Rwanda an
independent republic. This action embarrassed the United

Nations Trusteeship Council and Assembly by placing them in the position of appearing to deny and delay the independence of an African people. Nevertheless, suspicion of Belgian influence prevailed and the United Nations General Assembly declared that it was the duty of Belgium as administering authority to install "broad based" caretaker governments in both Rwanda and Burundi until legislative elections could be held in August 1961 under United Nations supervision. Subsequent plebiscites conducted under United Nations auspices resulted in the creation of two independent states, Rwanda and Burundi. In Burundi the predominant Batutsi retained political supremacy under the hereditary Mwami. Rwanda, however, staged a republican revolution placing power in the hands of the Bahutu majority. Subsequent exiling of large numbers of the aristocratic Tutsis has created tension between Rwanda and Burundi and endangered the peace of the area.

SEVEN

++++++++++++++++++++++++++

INTERNATIONAL ASPECTS

OF AFRICAN POLITICS

In closing this brief survey of internal political organization in Africa south of the Sahara, it is tempting to speculate on the international consequences of the emergence of modern states from the colonial and tribal societies of the region. Lord Hailey uses the term Africanism in preference to nationalism to describe the diverse forms that the impetus toward closer union linked with freedom from colonial domination has taken throughout the subcontinent.[1] This distinction stems from a depth of understanding that makes overcasual analogies between Western and African political experience unacceptable. Nationalism is, after all, a Western import which the awakening African masses may or may not find a suitable instrument for the realization of their hopes.

African intellectuals share with their Western teachers a predilection to impose personal views and feelings on the inchoate temper of the rising African masses. For example, the concept of "African personality" has tended to become a convenient vehicle for the esoteric speculations of an educated élite. We can, however, recognize inherent—even though sometimes conflicting—elements in the spirit of Africanism. On the one hand, a desire for cultural homogeneity unquestionably exists opposing itself to tribal, religious, linguistic, and geographical barriers between peoples. To some enthusiasts this foreshadows a pan-African movement that will unite Black Africa under the banner of one race, one people, one state. On the other hand practical political developments have lain in the direction of geographical and tribal combinations dictated by the exigencies of power. It is probable that the nation-state must be achieved before the continental state can be envisaged.

Economic pressures stimulate the growth of Africanism as against narrow nationalisms. Divided into isolated cultural groups, Africans face material deprivations that bar them from most of the benefits of modern life. In order to overcome obstacles of impoverished soil and poor communications, a far greater degree of social coöperation is required in tropical Africa than on Western continents. This economic motive transcends ethnic and political separatism. In fact the European element, both governmental and settler, has richly contributed to this aspect of Africanism. As a British authority on African economics, Professor Herbert S. Frankel, points out:

The subsistence economics of Africa still dominate the economic pattern of the newly independent States of Africa. In some even shifting cultivation is still necessary—others depend on sending their "surplus" labour far afield in search of work. As much as by lack of roads and railways and modern storage facilities, they are cut off by lack of knowledge and suitable techniques from meeting the requirements of distant markets. The real state of most of Africa is quite the reverse of that which most people unacquainted with it are apt to imagine. It is not an Africa "dependent" on Europe, but an Africa which over vast areas is cut off from the world economy: an Africa whose difficult task it is even to maintain the *status quo* in relation to the environment which only modern science and suitable forms of economic, political and administrative organization can eventually transcend. The real enemy of the African people is social and economic stagnation—and the perpetuation of, or return to, the isolation on which it rests.

He ["the new African"] is reaching out for a new "dependence," *i.e.* participation in and links with the modern world. In so far as the new African States fail to fashion those links, political independence will prove a mirage and will throw back their emergent populations to economic misery and chaos.[2]

Evidence of the contention that independent Africa desires rather than fears increasing degrees of economic integration with the Western world was forthcoming at the meeting of the European Parliament in June 1961. This recently formed offspring of the European Economic Community met with representatives from sixteen independent African states, fourteen from the areas of French expression together with Somalia and the Congo (Leopoldville), for the purpose of working out the future association of the African nations with the European Common Market. United African demands lay in the direction of continuation and augmentation of special tariff preferences, economic aid, and the stabilization of the prices of their tropical raw materials. Though observing the formalities of bilateral agreements between sovereign states, the African nations have made it clear that they speak as a virtual entity with similar if not identical voices. In July 1964, the Yaoundé Convention embodying tariff, trade, and aid agreements between six European members of the EEC and eighteen associated African states came into effect.

Africanism, then, may be accounted a force of perhaps greater international consequence than the sovereign independence of each of the discrete states. Uncertainty still reigns concerning the institutional forms in which this new force of Africanism will express itself on the world stage.

Inter-African Conferences. The All-African Peoples Conference convened at Accra in 1958 may be claimed to have culminated one historic phase of Pan-Africanism and inaugurated another more institutional development. Ghana, and its leader Nkrumah, dominated the Accra conferences through the prestige of independence, still denied at that time to the French-speaking peoples and to the emergent Nigerian nation. Hence the results of the All-African Peoples conferences were to an extent a continuation of the propaganda efforts of previous Pan-African congresses held outside African territory. However, the voice of African peoples on the verge of independence became more authoritative and responsible both as regards its international and African audience. In August 1959 the states then comprising the "African bloc" at the United Nations convened at Monrovia, inaugurating formal consultations for the formation of foreign policy on an all-Africa level. Realities of independence, however, presented insuperable obstacles to the maintenance of unity in external policies for the newly sovereign states. Two rival nuclei appeared as centers for the institutional unity of Black Africa. The Brazzaville bloc comprising twelve French-speaking African nations, met in December 1960, agreeing in general to sponsor a common foreign policy, to intensify economic and cultural coöperation, to create a permanent secretariat, and to pool diplomatic representation. The question of a unified common defense system was raised but left vague.

In contrast, if not in opposition to, the Brazzaville bloc the Casablanca Conference was held in January 1961 with Morocco, the United Arab Republic, Ghana, Guinea, and Mali as its participants. An ambitious "African Charter" was projected by this conference outlining the establishment of an African Consultative Assembly, committees to be responsible for political, economic, and cultural matters on a joint basis, and even the creation of an African Joint High Command.

Neither of these groupings were inclusive enough to implement a common policy or joint administration structures for the whole of Black Africa. Hence a more realistic conference was convened at Monrovia in May 1961 under the presidency of President Tubman of Liberia. Besides the twelve members of the Brazzaville bloc the participants were Tunisia, Ethiopia, Somalia, Liberia, Sierra Leone, and Nigeria. The addition of the English-speaking countries, particularly the 35,000,000 Nigerians, made this conference the most serious of all attempts to establish an institutional and policy base for close African coöperation. Because Ghana, Guinea, Mali, Morocco, the United Arab

Republic, and Sudan declined to participate, the conference fell thus far short of its goal of all African unity. However, under the skilled leadership of the prime minister of Nigeria the Monrovia Conference established practical bases for joint action that should prove attractive to the abstaining states when present passions and jealousies have cooled. In the first place pledges were exchanged on the principles of noninterference of African states in each other's internal affairs, condemnation of all subversive activities against established governments on the part of neighboring states, and the treatment of all states regardless of differences in wealth or numbers on the basis of sovereign equality. Technical committees of experts were appointed to prepare plans for economic, education, cultural, scientific, technical, communication, and transport coördination. This gave continuity to a movement inaugurated by the metropolitan European powers in 1954 when a Commission for Technical Coöperation in Africa south of the Sahara (CTCA) was formed from the pooled scientific resources of the major colonial nations. A need for the continued teaching of French and English as governmentally recognized languages was acknowledged, as well as efforts directed to the revival of an African cultural heritage.

With respect to a joint international policy it was agreed that all participating states would contribute material and moral assistance to hasten the end of colonial domination within African borders. South Africa's policy of apartheid was unanimously condemned and United Nations action supported in general. Portuguese suppression of Angolan rebels provoked the censure of the conference. The conference gave itself continuing institutional form by organizing as the "Organization of Coöperation of African and Malagasy States," attaching to the parent body a commission entrusted with the settlement of disputes, by peaceful means, between African states. It would appear that the Monrovian Conference envisaged an institutional structure for Black Africa similar in some respects to the Organization of American States, except of course that in the case of Africa there would be no dominance by a Western colossus.

In May 1963 the Heads of state of thirty-one independent African nations met at Addis Abbaba and established a charter for an "Organization of African Unity." An assembly of Heads of state of governments convening once a year will constitute the supreme body. A council of Ministers will meet bi-annually served by a permanent Secretariat functioning on a full time basis. The Charter appears to embody the more gradualist proposals for unity favored by a majority of states as against the extreme views associated with Nkrumah of Ghana. Though the Charter did not require dissolution of existing blocs, the French-speaking states grouped under the African and Malagasy Union decided to dissolve their organization as a political entity, retaining, however, an African and Malagasy Union for Economic Co-operation.

It is clear that the strength of Africa's voice in world affairs will depend on the ability of her component peoples to channel their views and actions through a joint institutional structure of this kind. So long as the numerous small nations remain separated one from the other in jealous blocs, opportunities to fish in troubled waters will prove too great for outside powers to resist.[3]

The British Commonwealth and French Connection. Ties with former metropolitan powers have not been wholly severed in the assertion of sovereign independence. Britain's African colonies became equal members of the Commonwealth family on achieving nationhood. Though Commonwealth status does not carry with it any commitment to support a common international policy it is far from being a merely formal association. In essence the Commonwealth is the largest and most elaborate consultative organization in the world. Consultation and exchange of information on diplomatic, economic, technological, and scientific matters occurs at all levels of political and administrative organization. Accordingly new African nations of British origin have at their disposal the pooled knowledge of the other Commonwealth nations from which to draw in the formation of their policies. Though their own national interests remain paramount, at least they operate within the international field in full understanding of the relevant facts. In addition to official Commonwealth ties, a pattern of economic, educational, and administrative association remains as a legacy from colonial days. Certainly national pride dictates that this close association be repudiated at least in part. However, a way of doing things that has worked in the past is difficult to terminate until a better method presents itself. Provided that the infra structure of colonial economic organization transforms itself with tact and proper respect for policies proclaimed by the new political rulers, there seems little reason to expect any serious rupture in the pattern of trade relations. Increased contact with trade and cultural organizations outside the British sphere will not necessarily reverse traditional links though it will stimulate competitive bidding for the economic and political good will of the African peoples. The willingness of African leaders to use Commonwealth machinery was demonstrated by the attendance of seven African Prime Ministers at the Commonwealth Prime Ministers' Conference of 1964. The Conference communique calling for sufficiently representative institutions before the grant of independence to Southern Rhodesia constituted a diplomatic triumph for African statesmanship.

A practical network of financial and technical aid remains as an operative link between the Africa of French expression and her former metropole. In theory, equivalent assistance could be supplied by other Western, or—as the case of Guinea has shown—Soviet sources. Habit, existing institutional frameworks, linguistic and cultural similarities make any such shift unlikely unless provoked by strong political reactions on either side. Developments leading to greater coöperation with France than experienced in colonial days are possible. The wider economic and political horizon of the European Economic Community provides opportunity for African peoples to coöperate on comparatively equal terms in the promotion of common interests. Choice is no longer restricted to the role of client state to a European overlord or the alternative of independent isolation; partnership on a voluntary basis has become feasible within the new extra-national organizations in the process of evolution.

The United Nations and Africa. A major aspect of the involvement of Africa in international affairs has been the increasing importance of the United Nations as a third force rivaling colonial hegemony in its reactions with indigenous movements. Inheriting the principles of trusteeship from the mandate system of the League of Nations, the emergent United Nations organization enlarged its scope and range by claiming a measure of supervision over all non-self-governing territories. A doctrine of international accountability for the treatment of dependent peoples has expanded from the interpretation of Chapter XI of the Charter to a point where the United Nations appears to be asserting final responsibility for the dissolution of all colonial connections. Trusteeship, in so far as Black Africa is concerned, has fulfilled its immediate function with the granting of independence to Togoland, the Cameroun territories, Tanganyika, Rwanda, and Burundi. Except as a potential instrument to bring pressure on the Republic of South Africa in the disputed case of South-West Africa, there appears no further need for the intervention of the Trusteeship Council in African affairs. A diminution of the importance of this administrative arm of the United Nations, deliberately balanced between administering and nonadministering powers, has coincided with a rise in the influence exercised by the General Assembly in the politics of non-self-governing territories. For some time a substantial majority of noncolonial members has dominated the attitude of the Assembly toward all problems arising out of conditions of dependency. At its fifteenth session in 1960

the General Assembly adopted a declaration on the granting of independence to colonial countries and peoples. This
declaration recommended the immediate transference of
all governmental powers to the indigenous inhabitants of
dependent territories, without reservations or distinctions
as to race, creed, or color, and in accordance with the
freely expressed will of the majority as to the degree of
independence and freedom they sought to enjoy. Naturally the major European powers with continuing colonial
responsibilities withheld their support from this declaration
and the United States chose to abstain. By this declaration
the deliberative arm of the United Nations placed itself in
open opposition to the continuance of existing colonial governmental forms anywhere in Africa. Executive and administrative arms, the Security Council and the Secretariat, were placed in an uneasy position under growing
pressure to implement the policy of the Assembly in practice under the doctrine of international accountability.

Direct intervention in the administration of existing African colonies by United Nations bodies appears to be foreshadowed by several resolutions adopted at the fifteenth
session in 1960. In the first place the right to define what
constituted a non-self-governing territory under the terms
of Article 73 (e) of the Charter was summarily removed
from the individual nations concerned and placed in the
hands of the General Assembly with the adoption of a
series of principles concocted by an *ad hoc* Committee of
Six. Further developments in debate indicated a strong intention on the part of the Assembly to create working
parties to determine specific dates for the achievement of
independence on the part of the remaining colonies. The
powerful Committee on Information from non-self-governing territories introduced proposals in 1960 which, if put
into practice, would give the United Nations an important
supervisory role in the day-by-day administration of colonial areas. The first recommendation was directed at the
preparation of indigenous personnel to replace European
administrators at all levels. Second, renewed claims were

made for full reports on political activities, though submission of such information is not required of the administering power under a strict interpretation of the Charter. Third, specific demands were made on colonial administrations to comply with certain principles laid down for the avoidance of race discrimination. Participation of the indigenous inhabitants in the economic and social life of the community was declared a major objective to be achieved in part by implementation of an equal right to vote, equal educational opportunities, and legal equality in employment opportunities. It is obvious that such policies could not be put into immediate practice within the remaining Portuguese possessions or without the subservience of existing régimes to the will of an international sovereign. An unanswered question remains as to the means by which effective enforcement of United Nations resolutions is to be accomplished. Though a majority of anticolonial powers appears assured at all times in the Assembly and perhaps even in the Security Council, the force exercised by such majorities is circumscribed by the degree of acceptance accorded somewhat novel doctrines of international accountability. Major powers on the ground in Africa—France, Britain, Belgium, Portugal—are, at the least, sceptical of the capacity of the United Nations to implement its decisions in a realistic manner. Theoretically the power of the Soviet bloc or the United States, singly or in conjunction, would suffice to impose an African solution determined by the United Nations. For this to eventuate, however, a major realignment in the present power structure of the world would be required.

Consequences of United Nations intervention in the affairs of the former Belgian Congo will, in all probability, be extended beyond solution of immediate problems. Establishment of a United Nations "presence" in the heart of Black Africa widens the scope of effective relationship between many areas of the world and the emergent African peoples. Hitherto metropolitan powers possessing colonial connections monopolized control of administrative structures, governmental and commercial, through which direct communication could be maintained with African society. Though Asiatic nations, particularly India, possessed strong interests based on the movement of their nationals and direction of their commerce, participation in African concerns had in the past been blocked by the overlordship of the colonizing powers. Now a foothold has been provided for the personnel of all nations in new administrative structures bolstering up insufficiently trained African cadres. It appears unlikely that this "internationalization" of external aid and contacts will terminate with the restoration of full powers to an indigenous Congolese government. Other and wider problems involving Portuguese Africa and perhaps South-West Africa threaten to involve the United Nations even more deeply in direct administration of African situations. Now that the colonial monopoly is finally shattered, penetration of the hinterland of African economics and politics may be achieved by many of the formerly excluded nations through the apparatus of the United Nations, more efficiently than by means of private diplomacy. To the African peoples the United Nations presents opportunities of increasing their effective influence well beyond what their actual economic or military potentials warrant. By the careful balancing of one world interest against another—an art in which African statesmen showed considerable aptitude during their colonial bondage—Black Africa is in a position to provoke profitable competition to contribute to her needed development. An organizational infra structure capable of compensating for many of the gaps left by the withdrawal of trained colonial technicians has been built up at least in skeleton form through the participation of international organizations such as World Health Organization (WHO), Food and Agricultural Organization (FAO), and UNESCO in the solution of problems presented by African society in transition. Though crippled at present by lack of adequate funds these international bodies present a more favorable appearance to their African clients than the charitable apparatus of individual nations. In an increasingly competitive struggle for good relations with the new African nations it is probable that purely nationalistic approaches will become suspect and that merit may be acquired, even by great powers such as the United States, through the channeling of funds through United Nations organizations. In the field of long-range planning the United Nations is already well-established through sponsorship of the principal regional economic body, the Economic Commission for Africa.

During the 1960 and 1961 sessions the United Nations interposed itself more directly between a colonial power and its African subjects than on any previous occasion. The question of Portuguese territories started in 1960 as an endeavor on the part of an Assembly majority to force metropolitan Portugal to acknowledge the colonial character of its possessions and submit reports to the United Nations under paragraph 73 (e) of the Charter. This of course was a preliminary step in the enforcement of international accountability which would have deprived Portugal of her claim to the sole determination of policies for her African possessions. Rebellion in Angola in 1961 enlarged the scope of United Nations action. Discussions in the Security Council and General Assembly led to the appointment of a committee by the Assembly to inspect and report on conditions in Portuguese Angola. Portugal refused entry to the committee and on June 9, 1961, the Security Council, "Having considered the situation in Angola, deeply deploring the large scale killings and the severely repressive measures in Angola, taking note of the grave concern and strong reactions to such occurrences throughout the continent of Africa and in other parts of the world, convinced that the continuance of the situation in Angola is an actual and potential cause of international friction and is likely to endanger the maintenance of international peace and security . . . Reaffirms General Assembly Resolution 1603 (appointing a Committee) and calls upon Portugal to act in accordance with the terms of that resolution; Requests the subcommittee appointed in terms of the aforesaid General Assembly resolution to implement its mandate without delay; Calls upon the Portuguese authorities to desist forthwith from repressive measures and further to extend every facility to the subcommittee to enable it to perform its tasks expeditiously. . . ." [4] This Security Council resolution was adopted by a 9 to 0 vote with Britain and France abstaining. Portugal can count only on the Republic of South Africa and Southern Rhodesia for toleration of her policies among African governments. Outside Africa, Spain would appear her sole active supporter. United Nations pressure, then, has good prospects of bringing about substantial changes in Portuguese Africa. Success in this area will encourage the independent African nations to build up a powerful grouping within the United Nations to attempt the internationalization of the South African question.

Relations of the Republic of South Africa to the rest of the continent constitute a major issue that must dominate the future politics of Africa. So long as the doctrine of white supremacy radiates from the southern tip of the continent to other areas of white settlement, African freedom remains precarious. Even the tacit consent of the major Europeans powers and the United States to South Africa's claim to treat race domination as an internal affair outside the scope of the United Nations must be treated as a hostile attitude by the African states. They can be assured that this viewpoint will receive support from the Asiatic countries, the Arab and Islamic nations, the Soviet bloc, and probably from Latin America. The present record of the United Nations in dealing with problems posed by South Africa over the last decade has been one of pious futility. In principle the Republic of South Africa has been condemned both for its race policies and for refusal to accept the obligation of international trusteeship in South-West Africa. Action to implement United Nations claims in respect to South-West Africa have become bogged down in juristic quibbling and virtual disregard of rulings by the International Court of Justice on the part of South Africa. A long succession of increasingly peremptory resolutions by the General Assembly on South African race policies have achieved nothing more than a grudging consent on the part of the South African government to receive the Secretary General of the United Nations for the purpose of informal conversations. Obviously the United Nations must act through power in order to influence the Afrikaner régime in South Africa.

Limitations on the future influence of the United Nations on the affairs of Africa south of the Sahara depend to a considerable extent on the handling of the South African question. It is unlikely that the independent states of Africa and their Arab and Asiatic sympathizers will continue to rely on an international body that acknowledges incapacity to intervene to alleviate the racial oppression practiced by the South African government. On the other hand, effective action by the United Nations would almost certainly require substantial economic sanctions to be enforced principally by the United Kingdom and the United States. Application of such sanctions would be politically unpopular among influential groups in both countries as serious disturbances in the investment market and perhaps in the supply of some needed minerals might eventuate from punitive measures against the South African economy. The degree to which either the United States or Great Britain supports the influence of the United Nations in Africa remains in doubt. Immediate policies indicate that for the United States the principal value of the United Nations in that region is to act as a barrier to intrusion by the Soviets. This is obviously a short-range policy. From the point of view of the United States the choice lies between selection of the United Nations as the principal instrument of American policy in Black Africa or the creation of a united Western policy to be implemented by a force equivalent to that placed at the disposal of the North Atlantic Treaty Organization (NATO). Neither alternative could be adopted as the policy of the American people without sharp debate and the sacrifice of many well-protected interests and many long-cherished concepts.

The continuity of the long-range interests of the United States in Africa south of the Sahara is insufficiently recognized. These interests predate the European "scramble for Africa" that followed the breakdown of the ostensible purposes of the Berlin Conference of 1886. An Open Door policy permitting equal opportunity of access to African resources and markets has been for the past century, and remains today, a major objective of American foreign policy. Supplementary to this concept is the ideal of an internal African economic structure integrating into social and economic union the widest possible region. The nineteenth-century dream of a "Congo basin" unifying the greater part of western and central Africa south of the Sahara embodied many American interests. Third, an international solution to the problem of bringing African communities within the fold of our technological culture has been consistently preferred over colonial tutelage by the American public and their statesmen. Finally the neutralization of Black Africa so that its territory and manpower does not become involved in inter-European wars has remained a consistent aim of the United States, an objective applicable to the present Cold War. In light of these clear-cut and well-established interests it appears regrettable that so little has been achieved during the past century toward formulating practical policies for their implementation. Because the African political situation is peculiarly vulnerable to external influences, the attitudes of the United States will prove a major factor in determining which among several potential manifestations will achieve actuality. It would be comforting both for the future of African culture and the security of the United States to prognosticate that United States policies would reflect the deep-rooted continuity of American interests. A rhetorical hope of this nature, however, must be qualified by a study of past failures to match contemporary policies with the long-range interests of the United States in sub-Saharan Africa.

APPENDIX

NOTES

BIBLIOGRAPHIES

APPENDIX

•••

THE NATIONS OF AFRICA
•••

NATION	DATE OF INDEPENDENCE
ETHIOPIA	*ancient times*
LIBERIA	*July 26, 1847*
REPUBLIC OF SOUTH AFRICA° (UNION OF SOUTH AFRICA)	*May 31, 1910*
UNITED ARAB REPUBLIC°° (EGYPT)	*February 28, 1922*
LIBYA	*December 24, 1951*
SUDAN	*January 1, 1956*
MOROCCO	*March 3, 1956*
TUNISIA	*March 20, 1956*
GHANA—c	*March 6, 1957*
GUINEA	*October 2, 1958*
CAMEROON	*October 1, 1960*
TOGO—f	*April 27, 1960*

° By a referendum in October 1960, the Union of South Africa became the Republic of South Africa on May 31, 1961.

°° The United Arab Republic was formed on February 1, 1958 when Syria joined Egypt. Syria withdrew from the United Arab Republic on October 5, 1961.

c—British Commonwealth
f—French Community

NATION	DATE OF INDEPENDENCE
MALAGASY REPUBLIC—f (MADAGASCAR)	June 26, 1960
REPUBLIC OF THE CONGO (LEOPOLDVILLE)	June 30, 1960
SOMALI REPUBLIC	July 1, 1960
DAHOMEY	August 1, 1960
NIGER	August 3, 1960
UPPER VOLTA	August 5, 1960
IVORY COAST	August 7, 1960
REPUBLIC OF CHAD—f	August 11, 1960
CENTRAL AFRICAN REPUBLIC—f	August 13, 1960
REPUBLIC OF CONGO—f (BRAZZAVILLE)	August 15, 1960
GABON	August 17, 1960
SENEGAL	August 20, 1960
MALI	September 22, 1960
NIGERIA—c	October 1, 1960
MAURITANIA	November 28, 1960
SIERRA LEONE—c	April 27, 1961
BURUNDI	July 1, 1962

NATION	DATE OF INDEPENDENCE
RWANDA	*July 1, 1962*
ALGERIA	*July 3, 1962*
UGANDA—c	*October 9, 1962*
KENYA—c	*December 12, 1963*
UNITED REPUBLIC OF TANGANYIKA AND ZANZIBAR***—c	*April 26, 1964*
MALAWI—c (NYASALAND)	*July 6, 1964*
ZAMBIA—c (NORTHERN RHODESIA)	*October 24, 1964*
GAMBIA	*tentative date, February, 1965*

*** On April 26, 1964 Tanganyika and Zanzibar merged to form the United Republic of Tanganyika and Zanzibar. Each had become independent previous to that date. Tanganyika was proclaimed independent on December 9, 1961, while Zanzibar gained independence on December 10, 1963.

NOTES

CHAPTER ONE

(1) Lord Hailey, *Native Administration in the British African Territories.* London, Colonial Office, H.M.S.O., 1951, Part IV, p. 2.
(2) The Political Constitution of the Portuguese Republic, Articles 134 and 135.
(3) *The Colonial Empire 1947-48.* London, Colonial Office, 1948 (Command 7433).
(4) The Hansard Society, *Debates in Parliament,* Vol. 477 (1386), London, 1950.

CHAPTER TWO

(1) Afrikaans was formerly regarded as a dialect of classical Dutch. It replaced Dutch as an official language of the Union on equal footing with English in 1925.
(2) This estimate is contained in an article by Professor Sadie of Stellenbosch University in *South African Affairs,* January 1955.
(3) A valuable account of the background of this Act may be found in Gwendolen M. Carter, *The Politics of Inequality,* New York, Praeger, 1958, Chapter 2.
(4) *New York Times,* December 11, 1960.
(5) The first job reservation decree under clause 77 of the Industrial Conciliation Act of 1956 affected some 35,000 non-European clothing workers. The action was protested by the South African Federated Chamber of Industries and by a strike of the European Garment Workers Union as destructive to the industry itself. For a contemporary report see the *Central African Examiner,* December 7, 1957.

(6) For a brief account of the Bantu educational system see J. W. Macquarrie, "The New Order in Bantu Education," *Africa South,* Oct.-Dec. 1956.

(7) In 1955 the number accused of law-breaking was 2,022,-480 out of a population of between 11 and 12 million.

(8) *The Economist,* London, June 4, 1960. Company reports.

(9) These principles are set out by the professor of Colonial Law and Administration at the University of Lisbon, Marcello Caetano, in "Principles and Methods of Portuguese Colonial Administration" (Colston Papers), London, Butterworth's Scientific Publications, 1950. See also M. Caetano, *Colonizing Traditions, Principles and Methods of the Portuguese.* Lisbon, 1951.

(10) An authoritative description of current Portuguese administration in its African provinces may be found in James Duffy, *Portuguese Africa,* Chapter XI. Cambridge, Harvard University Press, 1959.

(11) These and subsequent figures as to the ratio of civilized to uncivilized are taken from *Annuario Estatistico do Imperio Colonial,* 1946, and from the *Annuario Estatistico do Ultramar,* 1954.

(12) Professor Carter suggests that closer analysis of the official figures would reduce the number of true African *assimilados* to between 8,000 and 10,000. See Gwendolin M. Carter, *Independence for Africa.* 1960, pp. 99-100. New York, Praeger, 1960.

(13) Revelations concerning Portuguese treatment of African natives set forth in Marvin Harris, *Portugal's African Wards,* are to a considerable extent substantiated in the scholarly study of *Portuguese Africa* by James Duffy (see note 10).

(14) See Dr. Ade Sousa Franklin, "The Portuguese System of Protecting Native Landed Property," *Journal of African Administration,* January 1957.

(15) Sanford Berman, "Spanish Guinea," *Africa Report,* January 1961.

CHAPTER THREE

(1) For a detailed study by a social anthropologist of the history of this transition period in Nyasaland see J. A. Barnes, *Politics in a Changing Society.* New York, Oxford University Press, 1954.

(2) Thomas Franck, *Race and Nationalism,* p. 69. New York, Fordham University Press, 1960.

(3) *New York Times,* March 18, 1956.

(4) The color bar issue was settled about 1954-55 by negotiation with the European Union initiated by the Rhodesian Selection Trust Group. Opportunities were provided by which
Africans could gradually progress up a ladder of skills until
they qualified for European rates of pay.

(5) *African Report,* Vol. 5, No. 12 (December 1960).

(6) Thomas Franck, *op. cit.,* p. 121.

(7) Terence Ranger, "The Malawi Party," *Africa Special
Report,* Vol. 5, No. 8 (August 1960).

(8) *Indians in Kenya,* 1923 (Command 1922).

(9) *East Africa Royal Commission 1953-55 Report,* p. 14
(Command 9475).

(10) *Ibid.,* pp. 26-27.

(11) *Ibid.,* p. 146.

(12) *Report of the Kenya Constitutional Conference 1960.*
London, H.M.S.O., p. 6 (Command 960).

CHAPTER FOUR

(1) *East Africa Royal Commission Report,* 1955, p. 18.

(2) F. Burke, "The New Role of the Chief in Uganda," *Journal of African Administration,* Vol. X, No. 3 (July 1958).

(3) *The Colonial Territories 1956-57.* London, H.M.S.O., p.
20.

(4) F. Burke, *op. cit.,* pp. 157-58.

(5) Sir Andrew Cohen, *British Policy in Changing Africa.*
Evanston, Ill., 1959, pp. 58-59.

(6) *East Africa Royal Commission Report,* 1955, p. 349.

(7) For a full account see C. K. Meek, *Land Law and Custom in the Colonies.* 2nd ed. London, Oxford, 1949, Chapter
XII.

(8) *East Africa Royal Commission Report,* 1955, p. 368.

(9) *Report of the United Nations Visiting Mission to East
Africa* (T/218 and T/218 Add. 1), 1950, p. 76.

(10) See J. Gus Liebenow, "Tribalism, Traditionalism, and
Modernism in Chagga Local Government," *Journal of African
Administration,* Vol. X, No. 2 (April 1958).

(11) *The Times,* London, December 16, 1959.

(12) Julius Nyerere, "We Cannot Afford to Fail," *Africa Special Report,* Vol. 4, No. 12 (December 1959).

(13) *Ibid.*

(14) Lord Hailey, *An African Survey Revised 1956.* London,

1957, p. 501.

(15) *New York Times,* March 13, 1960.
(16) For a recent study of the interrelationships between Creoles and tribal Africans see Michael Banton, *West African City: A Study of Tribal Life in Freetown.* London, Oxford University Press, 1957.
(17) *The Gambia.* Report for 1956-57. London, H.M.S.O., 1958, p. 5.

CHAPTER FIVE

(1) *New York Times,* March 24, 1957.
(2) For more recent observations on the character of Monrovian society see Pierre and Renée Gosset, *L'Afrique, les Africains,* Paris, 1958, Vol. II, Chapter 11.
(3) *Ibid.,* p. 38.
(4) R. L. Buell, *The Native Problem in Africa.* New York, Macmillan, 1928, Vol. II, pp. 705-888.
(5) *Ibid.,* Vol. II, p. 707.
(6) *Ibid.,* Vol. II, p. 852.
(7) William Koren, Jr., *Liberia, the League and the United States.* Foreign Policy Reports. Vol. X, No. 19 (November 1934), p. 245.
(8) "Papers Concerning Affairs in Liberia," *British Blue Book* (Command 4614), London, H.M.S.O., quoted in R. Earle Anderson, *Liberia, America's African Friend.* Chapel Hill, 1952, pp. 122-23.
(9) William A. Hance, *African Economic Development.* New York, Harpers, 1958, p. 253.
(10) *Ibid.,* p. 229.
(11) Babatunde A. Williams, "Where Does Nigeria Go from Here," *Africa Report,* Vol. 5, No. 10 (October 1960).
(12) *Government Proposals for a Republican Constitution.* Accra, Government Printer, 1960, p. 5.
(13) Ghana Information and Trade Center, press release, No. 65.3, New York (January 1961).
(14) *Ibid.,* No. 63.29 (December 1960).
(15) *Ibid.,* No. 66.4 (January 1961).

CHAPTER SIX

(1) The expression "French-speaking Africa" may be misleading unless qualified by the explanation that French, while

the lingua franca of the educated minority is not a common tongue displacing tribal dialects throughout the whole area.

(2) An excellent account of the working of the party system as it affected French West Africa up to February 1961 may be found in Thomas Hodgkin and Ruth Schacter, "French-Speaking West Africa in Transition," *International Conciliation*, Vol. 528 (May 1960).

(3) Quoted from Colin Legum, *Congo Disaster*. London, Penguin Books, 1961, p. 40.

(4) A representative sampling of such opinion may be found in the following titles: Colin Legum, *op. cit.*; Alan P. Merriam, *Congo, Background of Conflict*. Evanston, Northwestern University Press, 1961; Maurice N. Hennessy, *The Congo, A Brief History and Appraisal*. New York, Praeger, 1961; Edwin S. Munger, *Conflict in the Congo*, American Universities Field Staff Reports Service, "Central and Southern African Series," Vol. 8, Nos. 1-3 (August-September 1960); Fernand Van Langenhove, "Le Congo et les Problèmes de la Décolonisation," *Chronique de Politique Étrangère*, "La Crise Congolaise." Brussels, Institut Royal des Relations Internationales, Vol. 13, Nos. 4-6 (July-November 1960).

CHAPTER SEVEN

(1) Lord Hailey, *An African Survey Revised*, 1956. London, Oxford University Press, 1957.

(2) Herbert S. Frankel, "Economic Aspects of Political Independence in Africa," *International Affairs*, October 1960.

(3) A recent study of African diplomacy within the United Nations is Thomas Hovet, *Africa in the United Nations*, Northwestern University Press, 1963.

(4) *New York Times*, June 10, 1961.

BIBLIOGRAPHICAL NOTE

++++++++++++++++++++++++++

REFERENCE

Two major works, one British and one American, provide invaluable service as reference works among the recent flood of topical and specialized publications on Africa south of the Sahara:

Lord Hailey, *An African Survey Revised 1956. A Study of Problems in Africa South of the Sahara.* London, Oxford University Press, 1957.

George H. T. Kimble, *Tropical Africa.* 2 vols. New York, The Twentieth Century Fund, 1960. Also in paperback format.

GENERAL

Raymond L. Buell, *The Native Problem in Africa.* 2 vols. New York, Macmillan, 1928.

Gwendolen M. Carter, *Independence for Africa.* New York, Praeger, 1960.

Sir Andrew Cohen, *British Policy in Changing Africa.* Evanston, Northwestern University Press, 1959.

James Duffy and R. A. Manners, eds., *Africa Speaks.* Princeton, N. J., D. Van Nostrand, 1961.

Rupert Emerson, *From Empire to Nation.* Cambridge, Harvard University Press, 1960.

Walter Goldschmidt, ed., *The United States and Africa.* New York, The American Assembly, Columbia University, 1958.

Lord Hailey, *Native Administration in the British African Territories.* 6 vols. London, H.M.S.O., 1951-55.

Charles G. Haines, ed., *Africa Today.* Baltimore, Johns Hopkins University Press, 1955.

William Hance, *African Economic Development*. New York, Oxford University Press, 1958.

Thomas Hodgkin, *Nationalism in Colonial Africa*. New York, New York University Press, 1957.

W. J. M. Mackenzie and Kenneth Robinson, *Five Elections in Africa, A Group of Electoral Studies*. Oxford, Clarendon Press, 1960.

W. M. Macmillan, *The Road to Self-Rule*. London, Faber and Faber, 1959.

K. M. Panikker, *The Afro-Asian States and Their Problems*. New York, John Day, 1960.

Anthony Sampson, *Common Sense About Africa*. New York, Macmillan, 1960.

Ndabanigi Sithole, *African Nationalism*. London, Oxford University Press, 1960.

INDIGENOUS SYSTEMS OF GOVERNMENT

W. R. Bascom and M. J. Herskovits, eds., *Continuity and Change in African Cultures*. Chicago, University of Chicago Press, 1959.

J. A. Barnes, *Politics in a Changing Society*. London, Oxford University Press, 1954.

Paul Bohannan, *Justice and Judgment among the Tiv*. London, Oxford University Press, 1957.

T. O. Elias, *The Nature of African Customary Law*. Manchester, Manchester University Press, 1956.

Lloyd A. Fallers, *Bantu Bureaucracy: A Study of Integration and Conflict in the Political Institutions of an East African People*. Cambridge, Heffer, 1956.

M. Fortes and E. E. Evans-Pritchard, eds., *African Political Systems*. London, Oxford University Press, 1940.

Simon and Phoebe Ottenberg, eds., *Cultures and Societies of Africa*. New York, Random House, 1960.

Audrey I. Richards, ed., *East African Chiefs, A Study of Political Development in Some Uganda and Tanganyika Tribes*. New York, Praeger, 1960.

SOUTH AFRICA

E. H. Brookes and J. B. Macauley, *Civil Liberty in South Africa*. Cape Town, Oxford University Press, 1958.

Gwendolen M. Carter, *The Politics of Inequality*. New York, Praeger, 1958.

S. Pienaar and Anthony Sampson, *South Africa, Two Views of Separate Development*. London, Oxford University Press, 1960.

Hector Monteith Robertson, *South Africa, Economic and Political Aspects*. Durham, Duke University Press, 1957.

PORTUGUESE AFRICAN POSSESSIONS

James Duffy, *Portuguese Africa*. Cambridge, Harvard University Press, 1959.

WEST AFRICA OF FRENCH EXPRESSION

Thomas Hodgkin and Ruth Schacter, "French-Speaking West Africa in Transition," *International Conciliation*, Vol. 528, May 1960.

Official Publications of French West Africa 1946-1958. A Guide. Compiled by Helen F. Conover. Washington, D. C., Library of Congress, 1960.

Virginia Thompson and Richard Adloff, *French West Africa*. Also *Emerging States of French Equatorial Africa*. Stanford, Stanford University Press, 1958 and 1960.

THE CONGO (LEOPOLDVILLE)

Info Congo, *Belgian Congo*. Translated by F. H. and C. Heldt. 2 vols. Brussels, 1959.

Colin Legum, *Congo Disaster*. Baltimore, Penguin Books, 1961.

Alan P. Merriam, *Congo, Background of Conflict*. Evanston, Northwestern University Press, 1961.

ENGLISH-SPEAKING WEST AFRICA

James S. Coleman, *Nigeria, Background to Nationalism*. Berkeley, University of California Press, 1958.

L. Gray Cowan, *Local Government in West Africa*. New York, Columbia University Press, 1958.

K. Ezera, *Constitutional Development in Nigeria*. New York, Cambridge University Press, 1960.

J. D. Fage, *An Introduction to the History of West Africa*. Cambridge, Cambridge University Press, 1959.

Kenneth Ingham, *The Making of Modern Uganda*. London, Allen and Unwin, 1958.

Roy Lewis, *Sierra Leone: A Modern Portrait*. London, Colonial Office, 1954.

Kwame Nkrumah, *Ghana: The Autobiography of Kwame Nkrumah*. New York, Thomas Nelson and Sons, 1957.

Nathaniel R. Richardson, *Liberia's Past and Present*. London, Diplomatic Press and Publishing Company, 1960.

Hugh B. and Mabel Smythe, *The New Nigerian Elite*. Stanford, Stanford University Press, 1960.

E. J. Yancy, *The Republic of Liberia*. London, Allen and Unwin, 1960.

EAST AND CENTRAL AFRICA

B. T. G. Chidzero, *Tanganyika and International Trusteeship*. New York, Oxford University Press, 1961.

Thomas M. Franck, *Race and Nationalism: The Struggle for Power in Rhodesia-Nyasaland*. New York, Fordham University Press, 1960.

Official Publications of British East Africa. Part One. Compiled by Helen F. Conover. Washington, D. C., Library of Congress, 1960.

GOVERNMENT REPORTS

United States.

Development Program in Africa South of the Sahara. Staff study No. 8. Subcommittee on Technical Assistance Programs, Senate Committee on Foreign Relations. 84th Congress, 2nd Session, 1956.

Report of the Special Study Mission to Africa South and East of the Sahara, by Hon. Frances B. Bolton. House of Representatives Committee on Foreign Affairs. 84th Congress, 2nd Session, 1956.

United States Foreign Policy, Africa. A study directed by Melville Herskovits for the Senate Committee on Foreign Relations of the United States. 86th Congress, 1st Session. Comm Print, USGPO, 1959.

United Kingdom.

Colonial Annual Reports: *Bechuanaland Protectorate 1958.*
Basutoland 1960.
Kenya 1958.
Northern Rhodesia 1959.

> *Sierra Leone 1960.*
> *Tanganyika* Part 1, 1959.
>   Part 2, 1960.
> *Uganda 1960.*
> London, Colonial Office.

East Africa Royal Commission 1953-55 Report. Cmd. 9475, London, H.M.S.O., 1956.

Report of the Advisory Commission on the Review of the Constitution of Rhodesia and Nyasaland (Monckton Report). Cmd. 1148, London, H.M.S.O., 1960.

Report of the Constitutional Commissioner, Zanzibar, 1960, by Sir Hilary Blood. Zanzibar, Government Printer.

JOURNALS AND PERIODICALS

Africa, International African Institute, London.

Africa Report, Washington, D. C.

Africa South in Exile, London.

Africa Today, American Committee on Africa, New York.

African Affairs, Royal African Society, London.

African Studies Bulletin, African Studies Association, New York.

Afrique-Action, Tunis.

Afrique Nouvelle, Dakar, Senegal.

Central African Examiner, Salisbury, Southern Rhodesia.

Ghana Today, Accra, Ghana.

East Africa Journal, Nairobi.

Journal of African Administration, African Studies Branch, Colonial Office, London.

Journal of African History, Cambridge, England.

Journal of African Law, London.

Makerere Journal, Makerere, Uganda.

Overseas Quarterly, Department of Education in Tropical Areas, University of London Institute of Education, London.

Présence Africaine, Paris.

Problemes Africains, Revue de Presse Hebdomaire, Brussels.

West Africa, Lagos, Nigeria.

SUPPLEMENTARY BIBLIOGRAPHY

American Society of African Culture, ed., *Pan-Africanism Reconsidered*. Berkeley, University of California Press, 1962.

Sophia R. Ames, *Nkrumah of Ghana*. Chicago, Rand McNally, 1961.

D. E. Apter, *The Political Kingdom of Uganda*. Princeton, Princeton University Press, 1961.

Paul Bohannan, *Africa and Africans*. Garden City, N. Y., The Natural History Press, 1964.

D. E. Carney, *Government and Economy in British West Africa*. London, Twayne, 1961.

Gwendolen M. Carter, ed., *African One-Party States*. Ithaca, Cornell University Press, 1963.

Denis V. Cowen, *Foundations of Freedom, With Special Reference to Southern Africa*. New York, Oxford University Press, 1961.

Mamadou Dia, *The African Nations and World Solidarity*. New York, Praeger, 1962.

James Duffy, *Portugal in Africa*. Cambridge, Harvard University Press, 1959.

Kalu Ezera, *Constitutional Development in Nigeria*. Cambridge, Cambridge University Press, 1960.

Walter Goldschmidt, ed., *The United States and Africa*. Rev. ed. New York, Praeger, 1963.

Melville J. Herkovits, *The Human Factor in Changing Africa*. New York, Knopf, 1963.

Thomas Hodgkin, *African Political Parties*. Baltimore, Penguin Books, 1962.

Thomas Hovet, Jr., *Africa in the United Nations*. Evanston, Ill., Northwestern University Press, 1963.

Colin Legum, *Pan-Africanism: A Short Political Guide*. New York, Praeger, 1962.

William H. Lewis, ed., *New Forces in Africa*. Washington, Public Affairs, 1962.

Vernon McKay, *Africa in World Politics*. New York, Harper & Row, 1963.

Kwame Nkrumah, *Consciencism*. London, Heinemann, 1964.

————, *I Speak of Freedom*. New York, Praeger, 1961.

Thomas H. Okuma, *Angola in Ferment*. Boston, Beacon, 1962.

Norman J. Padelford and Rupert Emerson, *Africa and World Order*. New York, Praeger, 1963.

Margery Perham, *The Colonial Reckoning*. New York, Knopf, 1962.

Philip W. Quigg, ed., *Africa. A Foreign Affairs Reader*. New York, Praeger, 1964.

Leslie Rubin and Pauli Murray, *The Constitution and Government of Ghana*. London, Sweet and Maxwell, 1961.

Philippa Schuyler, *Who Killed the Congo?* New York, Devin, 1962.

Ronald Segal, *African Profiles*. Baltimore, Penguin Books, 1962.

————, ed., *Political Africa: A Who's Who of African Political Personalities*. New York, Praeger, 1961.

Leopold Senghor, *On African Socialism*. New York, Praeger, 1964.

George W. Shepherd, *The Politics of African Nationalism: Challenge to American Policy*. New York, Praeger, 1962.

Immanuel Wallenstein, *Africa: The Politics of Independence*. New York, Vintage Books, 1962.

Jack Woddis, *Africa—the Roots of Revolt*. New York, Citadel, 1961.

I. William Zartman, *Government and Politics in Northern Africa*. New York, Praeger, 1963.

OTHER RANDOM HOUSE STUDIES OF INTEREST

Studies in Economics

Studies in Sociology